Telling Fortunes By Cards

By CICELY KENT
With Many Diagrams

PUBLISHERS
SMALL, MAYNARD AND COMPANY
BOSTON

Kessinger Publishing's Rare Reprints
Thousands of Scarce and Hard-to-Find Books!

We kindly invite you to view our extensive catalog list at:
http://www.kessinger.net

Copyright, 1922
By SMALL, MAYNARD & COMPANY
(Incorporated)

Second Printing, March, 1924

Printed in the United States of America

THE MURRAY PRINTING COMPANY
THE BOSTON BOOKBINDING COMPANY
CAMBRIDGE, MASS.

CONTENTS

CHAPTER		PAGE
I.	PRELIMINARIES	11
II.	THE TARO	35
III.	MIXED COMBINATIONS	46
IV.	THE PACK	56
V.	DISPLAYING THE CARDS. EXAMPLE CASE NO. I	70
VI.	EXAMPLE CASES NOS. II AND III	86
VII.	TWO OTHER METHODS	97
VIII.	THE FOUR FANS	113
IX.	YOUR LIFE	122
X.	THE SHORT ENQUIRY	140
XI.	THE SMALLER CARDS	156
XII.	THE OUIJA BOARD	175

ILLUSTRATIONS

	TO FACE PAGE
PLATE I. (COLOURED)	72
PLATE II. (COLOURED)	87
PLATE III. (COLOURED)	91

	PAGE
THE MONTH'S EVENTS	98
THE CIRCLE OF TEN	106
THE FOUR FANS	115
YOUR LIFE	124
THE FOUR KNAVES	129
THE SHORT ENQUIRY	141
PAST, PRESENT, FUTURE	144
THE EIGHT-FOLD SIXES	170

TELLING FORTUNES BY CARDS

CHAPTER I

PRELIMINARIES

The General Theory of Divination by Cards. Everybody Clairvoyante. On the Eve of Psychic Developments and the World's New Order. Everyone able to Read His Own Future. A Word to the Sceptic. Forewarned is Forearmed. Shadows not Always Evil. How to Avoid Creating an Adverse Atmosphere. How to Receive Your Consultant. The Important Subject of Time in Relation to Divination.

No one knows the age in which cartomancy first began to be studied as an art. All we are certain of is that from time immemorial men and women have read the cards and through their symbolism striven to pierce the veil of futurity — and succeeded.

The methods described in most of the books we now possess are generally gathered from early works upon the subject. That which appeared simplest, and best suited to this age of rush and hurry, has been collected and brought up to date, without any thought of actual value and efficacy.

The methods described in this book are the results of actual human experience, extending over many years and generations of my own family.

It sometimes happens, one really does not know why, that a family is what is now called " psychic."

Generation after generation produces members who possess peculiar gifts of second sight, or second hearing, a tendency to premonition or divination.

What was in old times called " a wise woman " became a very treasured possession of a family. She was not only consulted by all her relatives, but by the whole countryside. In the annals of my family " wise women " have not been uncommon, and with their blood in my veins, a number of psychic faculties have come naturally to me, and I carry on many of my family traditions as a matter of daily routine.

No day passes that I do not read the cards, follow their advice, heed their warnings, and look eagerly and confidently forward to the good things they predict, which truly come to pass. Each day that I live brings me added confirmation that the future can be accurately foretold by this means. Is it therefore wonderful that I continue to consult them, or that I should be anxious to impart my methods to others?

The oracle which I consult is open to all inquirers. I merely indicate the manner in which it should be approached.

One of the greatest benefits derived from reading the cards is the enormous stimulus it gives to clairvoyance or second sight.

Please do not be dismayed on reading this and exclaim "But I have not second sight. I am not clairvoyante."

I can assure you that you are clairvoyante. Everyone is, whether they are aware of it or not. Some people are more so, some less so, but the faculty is in us all, and will develop more and more as this century progresses.

We are on the eve of enormous psychic developments. A new order of things is coming upon the world which will gradually recreate it. We are all growing sensitive to the invisible world around us.

At present when worried, or in doubt as to what particular course to pursue, you often seek the help of some reliable clairvoyante — a creature very hard to find, by the way. It is not that they are becoming extinct, or that they never existed. There are really more now than in any previous age, but the scientists snap them all up. When they get wind of a clairvoyante possessed of genuine powers, he or she is instantly placed outside the reach of the general public, and becomes a pampered darling to be used exclusively in the cause of scientific psychic research.

When you have mastered the system taught in this book, you will be your own clairvoyante. You will have no need to consult thought-readers or cartomantes. You will be in a position to read your own future with far greater accuracy than any stranger can do it for you.

Again you will be in a position to read the cards for any perplexed friend, either on

PRELIMINARIES

broad general lines, or by specialising on one particular event which seems likely to come to pass.

There are few people in this world who do not take a certain amount of interest in learning what is likely to happen to them in the future, and also in the futures of those with whom they are associated.

Even the rank unbeliever in the possibility of events being shown beforehand, by means of divination finds a certain amusement, if nothing deeper, in listening to predictions of future events, which he is convinced are evolved entirely from the imagination of the fortune-teller. He believes that the crystal, the cards, or whatever the method of divination employed, really amount to nothing more than a frivolous pastime which strives to be convincing. Despite this attitude, the sceptic often gets an enormous amount of satisfaction from the attempts to tell his fortune, and he is constantly compelled to admit that although what he has been told is " of course pure coincidence," it is extremely odd.

Sceptics do not realise how far more

marvellous it would be if all that is foretold by divination were indeed only " coincidence," and not the obvious and clearly marked pictures of what is about to happen in the future.

There are people who object on principle to the use of cards, or any other methods of revealing the future. To them it is wrong to pry into futurity. They shudder at the thought of tampering with what they consider to be suspiciously like witchcraft. Let us hope such timid souls will never meet with anything more likely to injure them than cartomancy.

Again, one often comes across people who are genuinely afraid of the cards and their revealings. Such persons have experienced a divination which was totally unexpected; and possibly rather disagreeable.

It must always be borne in mind that the cards convey warnings of trouble, as well as promises of happy events. Those who consult them must be prepared for this. " Forewarned is forearmed," and many an accident or difficulty can be safely avoided by remembering that " coming events cast their

PRELIMINARIES 17

shadows before." There is a very deep meaning lying at the root of this old saw.

The real power of the clairvoyante and the cartomante lies in her skill in interpreting those shadows. Second sight consists in seeing them, not in actually interpreting them.

Let us banish from our minds the conclusion that shadows are always evil. Daily experience ought to tell us this is not so. You do not regard your own shadow as evil, and you are grateful for the shadow of a tree in hot weather.

A girl friend of mine, who for long had been an earnest inquirer of the cards and had found their predictions of enormous help, suddenly, to my amazement, absolutely declined to handle them again. She also hated to see others touch them. She stated it to be her conviction that the cards brought bad luck, and in any case what they predicted was abominable. This girl was unprepared for the warning conveyed, and rather than take heed of the warning and avoid the danger she threw up the cards. Surely the sensible course to pursue would be to watch for the gathering clouds the cards predict, and seek shelter from the storm.

It is always gratifying to make converts, and the cards have a happy knack of doing this.

One expects the superior being, man, to be a sceptic; he usually is. Therefore it is charming when the cards tell him of important matters of which the humble reader of the cards can know nothing. More satisfactory still is it when the future events they indicate turn out to be substantially correct.

Quite recently I had the satisfaction of hearing a sceptic who consulted me exclaim: "It is really most remarkable and extraordinarily interesting." Only a few days before he had said, "Of course I don't believe in anything of the sort." Not paying particular attention to his attitude, I made no argument in favour of the cards, but very shortly after, he begged me to tell him about a prospective journey, and for a long time this unbeliever sat absorbed in the reading of his future.

PRELIMINARIES

I will here indicate one or two simple rules which every cartomante ought to follow if she desires to gain real success and proficiency.

It is a well-known fact that there are people for whom it is extremely difficult to read the future. Why such people ever consult the cards is something of a mystery. They create a difficulty by arriving with a firm determination to hear nothing that even approaches the truth. The interpreter of the cards feels this strong hostility, and it is apt to distract her attention from the business on hand.

The cartomante must be prepared to recognise this attitude of opposition, and endure it quite calmly. Her duty is simply to concentrate her mind on the cards lying before her, and interpret them as shortly and concisely as possible. She will probably be rewarded by the speedy return of her visitor with a demand for further information.

Again, there are times when the cards themselves seem to be at enmity with their reader, and even with each other. They resolutely defy all attempts to form intelligible statements from their appearance. They suggest the obstinate mood of a naughty child, and display it in a most provoking manner.

When the cards are hard to read, when they have little sequence and are muddled in their meanings, it will be found, as a rule, that it is the cartomante's own fault, or misfortune.

She is creating an adverse atmosphere by reason of her own disturbed thoughts.

Perhaps she is worried or despondent, tired or irritable. This troubled aura, or atmosphere, is forming such a thick and murky cloud around her and her consultant, that, naturally, the cards are infected by the gloomy thought waves being exhaled. The results, muddled cards, and inability to give a clear reading of them.

Personally I always find it a great mistake to sit close to the consultant while she shuffles the cards. When we are seated close together, I invariably recognise as belonging to me certain indications thrown up in the reading. I have proved this over

PRELIMINARIES 21

and over again. If you want to read a future clearly and accurately occupy yourself with something else whilst the consultant shuffles.

Suppose that some one I know is very much in my thoughts, and that certain events are likely to happen to us both in the near future. These events are practically certain to come out clearly in the cards, even though they are totally unknown to the one who has consulted me and is shuffling unless I move right away from her and deliberately change my thoughts.

If your mind is in a fussy or worried state, it is wisest to leave the room for two or three minutes, and return when your client has shuffled.

Such advice may seem trivial, but those who wish to read the cards clearly and truthfully will do well to follow it.

In a calm, normal state of mind, when nothing particular is claiming the attention, it is a good plan to sit down quietly at a short distance from your visitor and, while she shuffles, fix your mind upon her. Try to forget everything except the fact that the cards are the means of interpreting all that she desires to know, and that it needs concentration on your part to make that interpretation clear.

Upon no account talk to your consultant, or permit her to talk whilst shuffling. Subjects used in discussion at such moments, invariably come into the cards and cause a muddle. It is her future that you want to see thrown up by the cards, not the trivial passing events of the moment.

The person who keeps chattering, or thinking of first one subject then another whilst shuffling, is sure to have a vague unsatisfactory reading. This is disappointing alike to consultant and reader.

There are two or three ways of reading the cards in which it is necessary to fix the mind exclusively on one particular point, say, on one person about whom you wish for information. These ways will be explained further on. Apart from these exceptions, it will be well to keep the mind as much a blank as possible. That is if you desire the cards to give you the best results.

Feel confidence in your own methods,

PRELIMINARIES 23

or in the methods of those from whom you learn. They have long experience behind them. A half-hearted, or not wholly believing attitude towards the cards will not bring you much success in reading them.

As you become accustomed to interpret the various combinations of the cards, you will, of course, discover many new meanings for yourself. Many volumes would be required to set down all the various meanings now known to be correct.

It is important to be quite clear in your own mind as to the meanings of the cards. Therefore it is wisest to study one book and not many different works. Always read from the cards exactly what you see before you, however improbable that reading may appear when applied to a consultant. On no account attempt to fit in what you may know of her with cards that present in some combinations a totally different meaning. A reading that you see lying before you may appear wildly improbable, and totally at variance with what you know of your consultant. Pay no heed to this. Your business is to read exactly what you see. Simply that and nothing more. Give your interpretations quite apart from any attempt to reason how such a condition or circumstance can apply to the consultant. The cards know a great deal more than you do. There is always something fresh to be learned from each " fortune " you read.

For instance, suppose the cards show quarrelling and discord in a family you have always imagined to be a model of peace and harmony. Would it not be futile to give a reading in accord with your imagination, when the cards plainly show you a totally different condition of affairs?

This is only a warning instance of what might occur between reader and consultant. There is no temptation of private beliefs leading you away when the consultant is a stranger.

Do not be discouraged if you have failure, and if sometimes the cards do not tell you correctly of coming events. There are certain to be mistakes to begin with. You must gain proficiency which you cannot expect to attain at once.

Persevere and do not be nervous. The

most advanced clairvoyantes make mistakes in their predictions. The language of symbolism can never be easy. You are dealing with a science which is still in its earliest infancy, and one that can be developed to an unlimited extent.

To read the cards and interpret their meaning, is naturally much easier for those who are born strongly clairvoyante than it is for those less gifted.

Remember this, the more automatic and detached you are from outside thoughts, the more accurate will be your reading.

I do not say that this advice is easy to follow. It is not. The mere arrival of someone to consult you brings a flood of new thoughts and ideas. If she be a stranger you will speculate about her. If she be known to you, instantly you will remember familiar things in connection with her. Such erratic thinking must be curbed. The mind must be brought under control so far as it is humanly possible to do so.

I will now deal with a question which is very often put to me. It is a cause of deep perplexity to many a cartomante.

"What should I do if, when reading the cards, I come across some terrible disaster, or some very sad fate awaiting my consultant?"

My advice is, use your own judgment. I am against withholding facts of a sad nature; but when possible they ought to be passed lightly over. An approaching accident ought always to be mentioned. Forewarned is forearmed. Even a threatened illness may be avoided by strength of will, or ordinary precautions.

As a rule you will find that the good indications presented by the cards far outnumber the bad. Though many may deny it, in this world good outweighs evil. We are progressing upwards, despite the sinister tones thrown daily upon events by pessimistic journalists.

It is very unpleasant to be "a speculator for the fall," although your rule must be to state what you see, always remember that much depends on how the cards are placed, and the counting of them. I fully explain this further on.

The cards may appear at first glance to

come out very badly for a consultant, but on closer examination of surrounding cards, the bad news may not be entirely personal. Much of the trouble indicated may have no bearing on the individual state of affairs. It may have to do entirely with some knowledge of evil dwelling in the subconscious mind of the consultant.

For example, a friend of mine once witnessed a terrible fire, in which several people were trapped in their rooms and burned to death. For years afterwards she was haunted by a fear of being burned to death. This dread of fire invariably passed its message over whilst she shuffled the cards. Needless to say warning of death by fire appeared in the readings. A warning which of course, in her case she knew how to discount.

Do not therefore be dismayed if, at first sight, the cards appear bad and full of tragedy. By the various countings it may turn out that the evil aspects are nothing worse than public news absorbed from the daily papers, with which the mind of the consultant is saturated. Again, it may be that some tragedy told her by a friend is haunting her waking consciousness.

It must always be remembered how impersonal some readings may turn out to be and how unwise it is to jump to conclusions and give to events an entirely personal interpretation.

Upon one impersonal subject the cards never fail to be correct. I refer to the state of the weather, which presents itself in every reading. It is a strange fact which every cartomante must have noticed. The cards are absolutely correct weather prophets. Indeed, they are far more reliable than the sometimes erratic weather-glass. They know all about rain, change of wind, fogs, gales, etc., and tell you so with unerring precision.

Now, I wish to say a few words on the very important subject of time.

Personally, I hold that when reading a fortune it is far better to confess frankly that — as a rule — it is next to impossible to give a precise date. The reason is, that time, being a purely human institution, does not exist in clairvoyance.

Whilst you think of the present, it is past ere you can grasp it.

Now events shown in the cards may be, indeed often are, a considerable distance ahead, sometimes as much as a couple of years. The shadows cast by coming events are often very long ones, and we know very little of the laws which govern them.

Sometimes you will find that a certain event keeps coming up in the count, and constitutes itself the predominating feature of the reading.

The majority of cartomantes hold this to mean that the event is quite near. They are often wrong in this reading. I have known cases where all the signs pointed to a speedy culmination; yet the event did not come to pass for two years.

I do not wish for a moment to imply that the time of an event, occurrence, or condition is never shown. I only desire to point out that in reading the cards, time definitely indicated is the exception rather than the rule.

Naturally, your consultant will press you for a date. Let us suppose that she is a stranger to you, and that you see marriage in her cards. For all you know to the contrary, she may have fixed her wedding day for the following morning. In that case the cards would be so full of the coming event, that you would probably be driven into saying " your marriage will take place immediately."

On the other hand, the marriage day may be fixed for the following week, then something may intervene which will cause a very long postponement.

A friend of mine, skilled fortune-teller, was consulted in 1916 by the daughter of a well-known earl and diplomatist. My friend recognised the girl from her portrait, which had appeared the week before in a pictorial paper. Alongside her portrait was that of her lover, a young soldier. Their very important wedding was announced to take place in a month's time.

To her dismay my friend could find no indication of marriage on the cards. There was tragedy and death, but no sign of joyful wedding bells.

Minimising as well as she could the adverse

signs, she stated what she saw, to the obvious perplexity of her consultant. On rising the girl said: " I think I ought to tell you that you have failed badly with me. I am going to be married in a week's time." Two days after her lover was killed at the front.

In 1918 the same girl came again to consult my friend, who recognised her instantly, though no name was given, nor was any reference made to that previous meeting.

This time the cards were saturated with marriage. My friend frankly said that, although it was risky to give dates, it was hard to avoid the conclusion that the wedding was imminent. " Indeed," she added, " though the cards do not actually say you are married, the ceremony might according to all indications be fixed for to-day."

The girl laughed and produced a wedding ring from her pocket. " I was married this morning quite privately. You will read it in to-morrow's papers," she said.

The most satisfactory method of arriving at a probable date is to predict what your impression of it tells you will be the time.

Intuition is the best method to use in dealing with the time element. Past, present, future are all one in the vision of the real clairvoyante. What is, has been, and will be form one vast picture visible as a whole.

The arbitrary division of time into days, weeks, years, has no part in the existence of the subconscious knowledge within us, which contains the eternal memory and can foresee the future. Time is necessary for the regulation of our everyday life, but it is swallowed up in eternity, which knows neither beginning nor end.

When considering the question of time in connection with an event, your inherent second sight will very probably tell you by means of symbolism what you wish to know.

Supposing you are dealing with marriage, which is strongly shown on the cards. You naturally desire to know when it will take place. That is the moment to be ready for clairvoyance by symbols. A patch of snow may float into your mental vision.

PRELIMINARIES

You may regard it as most probable that the marriage will take place in the winter. Or it may be that you suddenly get a whiff of the perfume of June roses, in which case the marriage will be a summer one.

Do not lightly disregard such signs or symbols, and cast them out of mind as mere foolish tricks of the imagination. They may be, and probably are quite as real and authentic as "God Save the King," which you can hum through from beginning to end, and repeat word for word in the depths of your mind and with closed lips, and without uttering the faintest whisper.

Remember that what you are pleased to call rather slightingly your imagination, is the cause of all the great discoveries the world has ever known.

With some cartomantes the correct date often comes in a flash and by instinct. It is more often than not an accurate forecast. Again, there are undoubtedly some events whose dates cannot be foretold, simply because the Powers that be have not decided when they shall begin or end.

The great war furnishes a good example of what I mean. Undoubtedly in that case coming events for long had been casting mighty shadows before, but who could foretell the psychological moment when the first shot would be fired?

Out of all the vast number of prophecies made by well-known clairvoyantes as to when the end of the war would come, so far as I know not one of them prophesied November 11th, 1918.

Whilst making predictions from cards, the seer will often receive distinct mental impressions that are not apparent in the cards themselves. Probably in some subtle way such impressions are produced by the cards — though not actually shown. They should therefore be given and included as a part of the interpretation of the whole reading.

CHAPTER II

THE TARO

The Taro the Oldest Form of Cards. Where the Taro Cards can be obtained. The Real Meaning of the Taro Still Kept Secret. Their Profound and Hidden Significance Still Jealously Guarded. Three Ways of Placing the Taro Cards. The Body, Soul and Spirit of the Taro.

BEFORE proceeding to describe the different combinations and methods of reading the cards, I will say a word or two upon the origin and symbolism of the Taro pack.

No card book would be complete without some reference to the oldest form of cards that has been handed down to us, more especially as they are now in constant demand, the interest in them having revived enormously.

Packs can now be obtained at the office of *The Occult Review*. They are in two styles, described respectively as *une tete* and *deux tetes* (one head and two heads). The difference is that the one head set is not reversible, the honours facing one way only, whereas the two heads pack is similar in style to the ordinary pack — the card being the same whichever way it is turned up.

The Taro form a study so very abstruse and difficult and so wholly apart from the cards which we commonly use, that I will not enter into the intricacies of their divination. I will merely indicate a few facts connected with them, as there are numerous people who possess a positive genius for dealing with all methods of using cards. They are experts from the first hour in which they handle them, and to such the Taro may strongly appeal.

This is a point to remember in buying a card book for a friend. What may seem almost incomprehensible to you, may very probably be child's play to him or her. It is much the same in dealing with astrology. Casting a horoscope is a very simple matter to some folk, but impossible to others.

THE TARO

Authorities tell us that the Taro can be traced straight back to Atlantean times. "There were giants upon the earth in those days," says the Bible, and upon Easter Isle, lying in the Pacific off the coast of South America, which forms the last remaining portion of the submerged continent of Atlantis are to be found statues of giants, and the remains of a people immeasurably more advanced in occult lore than we are.

Other authorities maintain that the Taro are the earliest edition of our playing cards, and that both came from India. What seems most probable is that the Chaldean and Egyptian Initiates received the Taro from Atlantis, and eventually, in somewhat altered design, they have descended to us.

Though the Taro provide a marvellously interesting study, their real meaning has always been kept secret, and may not filter through into the world for centuries to come.

Their profound and hidden significance is still jealously guarded by certain Hermetic Schools, by oriental and occidental initiates, and by the Brotherhood of the Great White Lodge.

It is known that the Taro cards actually hold the wisdom of the ages, that they formed parts of the mysteries revealed to the candidate during initiation, and that their symbolic pictorial designs express and preserve profound spiritual truths, which the great majority in this world are not yet fitted to receive.

During the course of ages, some of the minor secrets which those cards enfold, have filtered through to the knowledge of occult students. They are now being dealt with, and intelligently studied in conjunction with what has come down to us from ancient writers of the 13th and 16th centuries.

The Egyptians, and other historic peoples, engraved on plates certain pictorial designs, which preserved, yet veiled, great spiritual truths. Ultimately those plates were used as cards. One authority, Swainson, states that from them were derived our playing cards. They were called by the Egyptians the Royal Path of Life. In Egyptian "Tar" means path, and "Ro" royal, hence Taro. The same authority states that their meaning is based on astrology.

THE TARO

The ordinary Taro pack consists of seventy-eight cards, but there are others besides the seventy-eight which embody still deeper truths. Only after the seventy-eight have been mastered, can those which are more profoundly sacred be studied with any hope of success.

This pack of seventy-eight cards is made up of four suits, namely pentacles, sceptres, cups and swords, corresponding respectively to diamonds, clubs, hearts and spades, fifty-six in all. There are also twenty-two trump cards, each bearing a different design.

The forty numbered cards are called the Minor Arcana. The sixteen Court cards, four in each suit, namely, King, Queen, Valet and Courtier, are called the Court Arcana. The twenty-two trump cards are named the Major Arcana. Every plane of being is in correspondence with these cards, and each has a definite spiritual meaning.

The four suits originally consisted of roses, trefoils, cups and acorns, which later were changed to pentacles, sceptres, cups and swords. Amongst other things they typify the four seasons, Spring, Summer, Autumn, Winter, the four fixed zodiacal signs, Aquarius, Leo, Scorpio and Taurus, representing earth, air, fire, water. They also correspond to the four forms of the sphynx, the man, the lion, the eagle, the bull.

The most important cards are the twenty-two Major Arcana, which correspond with the ten planets of the chain, seven active, three latent and the twelve signs of the zodiac.

I append a description of the Taro which years ago was given to me by an expert.

THE TARO

There are three ways of placing the Taro cards, which may be considered the Body, Soul, and Spirit of the Taro.

The first manner relates to the lower plane, and has reference to questions concerning everyday life, domestic matters, illness and simple queries, etc. For this placing the four Aces and their relative cards are only to be used.

The second manner has relation to Science, Philosophy, Religion, etc. For this, the Aces, with their cards, and the twenty-two keys are to be employed.

For the third manner of placing the Taro, the twenty-two keys only are to be used with the four Aces. The cards are to be left out entirely. This mode is to be used when the knowledge sought for is assignable to the Divine Wisdom, and the revelation and unfolding of the inner light, the sacred knowledge of the Occult.

To place the cards in position, the Aces are to be separated from the pack and shuffled by themselves, and are placed face downwards in the centre of the twelve positions, in the order A, B, C, D; the other cards are then to be placed as they arise in the positions numbered consecutively 1 to 12; in all cases face downwards.

The four Aces in the centre form always the Astral key of the knowledge sought for, and each card of the Astral key is allied to the trine of cards which cover the places having the same colour.

The colours were given to show the meaning

of the twelve places, and this meaning is intensified or weakened, elevated or lowered, according to the kind of knowledge desired.

The twelve places or thrones are divided into four trines; each of the places of the trine bears harmonious relationship to the other.

The meaning of the portions of the Aces which form the Astral key is as follows:—
A, coloured Red, is the throne of Motion, Action, Will, the proper throne for the Ace of Diamonds. This part of the key gives action to the Red trines numbered 1, 6, 11, and will powerfully affect it, if Diamonds fall on the place A.

The Red trine is the trine of life.

No. 1 is Present Existence, Action, Being, the Present State or Time.

No. 6 is Life in the Deity, the Source, the Creator.

No. 11 is Life in Posterity, Children, the After-course.

The second trine is coloured Yellow, and means power, influence, might, and to it belongs that part of the Astral key which

THE TARO 43

bears the same colour, marked B. The Ace of Clubs is the most powerful occupier of this Throne. No. 2 of this trine is the place of power, attached to Honour and Majesty.

No. 7. The power given by surroundings, connections, associations, intellect.

No. 12. The power and influence given by worth or material qualifications.

The third trine is coloured Green, and has the Ace of Cups as the bountiful and true occupier of its key — O. This is the trine of love, and the relative positions are numbered 3, 8, 9.

No. 3 is the place of love, felicity, agreement, delight.

No. 8 is love in service, reception, bounty.

No. 9 is the place of favour, help, succour.

The fourth place of the Astral key is marked D, and this with its relative trine signifies afflictions, oppositions, persecutions, punishment, according to the knowledge desired. It has for its significator the Ace of Swords. Should this ace fall on this throne of the key in a question of affliction or opposition, and swords also on the Violet trine, it would be very adverse.

The first place of this trine is No. 4, which is the throne of evil, sin, the pit, the casting down of the mighty retribution.

No. 5 is the place of malice, hatred, injury, treachery.

No. 10. The place of intellectual death, idiocy, mourning.

The common or ordinary meaning of the aces is: Diamonds — life; Clubs — power; Cups — love; Swords — affliction.

The meaning of their relative cards is according to their values, and the place and strength of the place where they may fall.

Diamonds. Signify and give life, satisfaction, ability, accomplishments, etc.

Clubs. Power, force, might, the creative will.

Cups. Love, beauty, pleasure, enjoyment, favour.

Swords. Affliction, illness, trial, testing, sifting and death.

When the cards have been placed on their thrones, faces downwards, that card of the

THE TARO

Astral key which will most particularly relate to the question, is first to be turned up, and the mind allowed to dwell on the bearings of this first page of revelation. The trine of cards that belong to this key is then to be shown, and the strength and meaning of the cards is to be read, with the meaning of the place or throne.

The key next in importance with its trine is then to be dealt with and so on with the rest.

Three different packs of cards should be employed, one kept particularly for the Divine Wisdom. This pack, when not used, should be placed away in a small cedar-wood box, wrapped in a linen cloth, and no hand but that of the student to be allowed to touch this pack.

CHAPTER III

MIXED COMBINATIONS

Predictions given from Cards to be Written Down. Combinations, What They Indicate. Time at which Meanings can be Verified.

CLUBS

KING OF CLUBS, ten of hearts — sincere affection. Ten of clubs (reversed). Seven of diamonds — a carriage and horse.

Ten of clubs, ten of diamonds — good luck.

Ten of clubs (reversed), knave of spades — an outing put off, or with accidents occurring to spoil it. Nine of clubs, knave of spades — a lawyer.

Nine of clubs, knave of spades, eight of diamonds — a policeman.

Nine of clubs, knave of spades, ace of spades — a will or legal document. Eight of clubs (reversed), nine of diamonds — a telegram.

MIXED COMBINATIONS

Eight of clubs, eight of spades — trouble about a great friend.

Eight of clubs (reversed), ace of spades — a meeting at a large building. Eight of clubs, nine of hearts — realised wishes, with regard to a great friend.

Ace of clubs, seven of spades, eight of diamonds — aeroplanes, doings in the air.

Ace of clubs, seven of diamonds — a parcel.

Ace of clubs, seven of diamonds (reversed) — a present or photograph.

Ace of clubs, knave of diamonds — surprising news.

DIAMONDS

Ace of diamonds, eight of hearts — an invitation.

Ace of diamonds, eight of hearts, knave of hearts — an engagement.

Ace of diamonds, ten of diamonds — a railway ticket.

Ace of diamonds, ace of clubs, knave of diamonds — a registered letter.

Ace of diamonds, seven of spades — shopping.

Ace of diamonds, eight of clubs (reversed) — a letter or papers about business.

Ten of diamonds, ace of spades — financial difficulties.

Ten of diamonds, ace of spades, ace of clubs (reversed) — difficulties with accounts.

Ten of diamonds (reversed), ace of spades — a railway station.

Ten of diamonds (reversed), ten of spades (reversed), ace of hearts — a fire.

Nine of diamonds, knave of spades — a doctor or dentist.

Nine of diamonds, eight of diamonds, seven of spades (reversed) — an accident on the road.

Nine of diamonds, ace of spades, knave of spades — an operation, with eight of spades touching the ace — at a hospital or nursing home.

Nine of diamonds, eight of diamonds — a bicycle.

Nine of diamonds, ten of diamonds (reversed), eight of diamonds — a motor car.

Nine of diamonds, ten of clubs (reversed) — a tram.

MIXED COMBINATIONS

Seven of diamonds, eight of diamonds — a horse.

Seven of diamonds, ace of clubs, eight of diamonds — a note, or papers brought by hand.

Seven of diamonds with a court card — present, brought by a person of the colouring indicated by court card.

Seven of diamonds (reversed), ace of spades — a bank.

Seven of diamonds (reversed), ace of spades, knave of spades — a bank manager.

Seven of diamonds, ace of spades — a school.

Seven of diamonds, ace of spades, eight of diamonds — a choir school.

Seven of diamonds, ace of spades, with club court card — a school-master or school-mistress according to the court card displayed.

Seven of diamonds, ace of spades, eight of spades, knave of spades, nine of diamonds — an epidemic at a school.

Seven of diamonds, king of spades — a book.

Seven of diamonds (reversed), seven of

clubs (reversed), ace of spades (reversed),— plans and changes causing annoyance. Seven of diamonds, seven of clubs — pleasant plans.

HEARTS

Ten of hearts, ace of spades — a birth.

Ten of hearts, ace of spades, eight of diamonds — a christening.

Ten of hearts, ace of diamonds, ace of clubs — banns of marriage.

Ten of hearts, ace of diamonds — a wedding.

Ten of hearts, ten of spades — frustrated happiness.

Nine of hearts, ace of spades — wishes and desires fulfilled.

Nine of hearts, ace of spades (reversed), knave of spades — ungratified desires.

Nine of hearts, nine of diamonds — wishes gratified with speed.

Nine of hearts, seven of spades, eight of diamonds — a wished-for change in the weather, good outlook.

Eight of hearts, seven of spades — new clothes.

Eight of hearts, seven of spades, ace of

hearts — new carpets or furniture, new paint or paper.

Eight of hearts, seven of spades with ace of spades touching—a draper's shop or dressmaking establishment.

Eight of hearts, eight of clubs (reversed)—pleasant meetings and talk.

Eight of hearts, knave of spades, ace of hearts — a broken engagement, or love affair with many obstacles.

Eight of hearts, eight of spades (reversed) trouble and heaviness through the affections.

Seven of hearts, ten or eight of spades — domestic difficulties and trials.

Knave of hearts, nine of hearts — happiness, great affection.

Knave of hearts, ten of spades—separation from one you love.

Knave of hearts, eight of diamonds, eight of spades — a meeting with a friend, or lover out of doors, resulting in a disagreement.

SPADES

Ace of spades, eight of diamonds — a church.

King of spades, ace of spades — a clergyman.

Ace of spades, ten of spades — a yacht.

King of spades, ace of spades, ten of spades, — a yachtsman.

Ace of spades, ten of spades, eight of diamonds — a harbour or pier.

King of spades, eight of hearts—a widower, or a man living apart from his wife.

King of spades, nine of clubs — a man of business.

King of spades, nine of diamonds — anger, feelings of wrath.

King of spades, nine of diamonds, eight of diamonds, ten of spades — thunder and lightning.

Ten of spades (reversed), eight of diamonds — rain; with ace of hearts — a fog.

Ten of spades (reversed), nine of diamonds — danger of drowning.

Ace of spades, eight of spades — a hospital or nursing home.

Ace of spades, eight of spades, queen of clubs — a nurse.

Ace of spades, nine of clubs — a theatre or concert hall.

Queen of spades, eight of hearts—a widow, or one living apart from her husband.

MIXED COMBINATIONS

Queen of spades, nine of diamonds — malicious tongues.

Ten of spades, ace of diamonds — loss of a valuable, or a breakage.

Ten of spades, ten of diamonds, with ace of spades touching—a battleship or destroyer.

Ten of spades, ten of clubs — a voyage, crossing the channel.

Ten of spades, eight of hearts — bereavement.

Nine of spades, nine of diamonds — death.

Nine of spades (reversed), ace of spades, eight of diamonds — a cemetery.

Nine of spades (reversed), ace of spades — a funeral.

Nine of spades, eight of diamonds — bad weather.

Nine of spades, eight of hearts—difficulties with those dear to you, shadowed friendship or love.

Eight of spades, eight of diamonds — lameness, discomfort in walking.

Seven of spades, eight of diamonds, ace of hearts — a gale.

Seven of spades, eight of diamonds — a change of wind or weather.

Several court cards coming together show social pleasures.

The eight of spades between court cards shows a quarrel, or disputing.

Eight of hearts between court cards — loyal friends.

Eight of clubs near hearts — new interests or work.

These various combinations of the cards will not be difficult to remember, if the separate meaning of each card is kept in view. The easiest way to learn them by heart is to lay out the cards indicated in the combined meanings; the eye then becomes used to them, and soon the meanings will be read in a flash. The aim of all who study the cards should be to make their card reading as mechanical as possible, to allow of the free exercise of the intuitive faculty so necessary to the divinatory interpretation of the cards.

It will be found most useful, as a help to this attainment, to take note of the various combined meanings which come in the cards, whether reading them for yourself or for others. The predictions given from

MIXED COMBINATIONS 55

the cards should be written down together with the cards representing those predictions, and in the exact order in which they are seen. It may be some months before all the meanings can be verified, but some may come at once. In any case it is most useful to have these notes for reference when in doubt as to any special meaning. The results as they occur, and are recognised, should be marked as correct or otherwise.

CHAPTER IV

THE PACK

The Ground Work and Alphabet of Learning and Interpreting the Cards. The Value of Suits. Combinations. What they Indicate. Significators. The Four Kings, the Four Queens and the Four Knaves. Colouring and Selection. Characters of Those Indicated by the Cards. A Hint to Those Not Gifted by Strong Clairvoyance. The Thoughts of the King and Queen Indicated by their Knaves. The General Meaning of Clubs, Diamonds, Hearts, Spades. Fours. Threes. Pairs.

THE PACK

THE complete pack of fifty-two cards is not necessary for the purpose of divination, although there are, of course, many ways of employing the whole. Four methods of using the fifty-two cards will be given in this book. The Bezique pack of thirty-two cards only is required in the method of laying out the cards we will now consider, and all twos, threes, fours, fives and sixes are taken out of the pack before being shuffled. The significance of

THE PACK

the four suits of the pack, and meanings of each of the cards therein, must be committed to memory before attempting card-reading. This is the ground work, and alphabet of learning for interpreting the cards, and no proficient readings can be done without thoroughly mastering it.

VALUE OF SUITS

Clubs. Position, authority, capacity for business, organisation, success.

Diamonds. Speed, finance, sharpness, rapidity in decision, precarious undertakings—dominated to a large extent by surrounding cards.

Hearts. Happiness, pleasure, the affections, domestic affairs, comforts.

Spades. Misfortunes, sorrow, mourning, distance, undoing, disappointments, tears, darkness, depression.

COMBINATIONS

Diamonds and clubs show successful business or monetary transactions, increase of prosperity.

Hearts and diamonds show pleasure, happiness, gaiety, enthusiasm, energy.

Diamonds and spades together are evil, showing danger, accident, illness, sometimes death.

Clubs and hearts show lasting affections, reliable natures, making good friends, constancy, truthful kindly disposed natures.

Clubs and spades denote things desired, difficult to obtain, remoteness, delays, thwartings, despondency, disappointments.

Spades and hearts show regrets, obstacles, unhappy marriages, unfortunate love affairs.

SIGNIFICATORS

The queens are used for women, according to their colouring, although, as there are only four queens, this number cannot represent the consultant, her family and friends, and each queen has to do duty for various people. The same rule applies to kings, who also are used to represent men of mature years, according to their colouring. Knaves or jacks are used for boys, messengers, also the thoughts of the kings and queens of the same suit. Some authorities say that wives should always take the colouring of their husbands, *e.g.*, the queen of spades consulting should take the king of spades to represent her husband, even if he were very fair, or had white hair. Personally, I find this unnecessary. It seems more reasonable to allow the fair man to be the king of diamonds, and the wife, being very dark, to retain her own colouring, the queen of spades. I find it answers very well to ask the consultant the colouring of her husband, and choose the king to represent him in accordance with that colour.

Diamonds denote people with white, red, or very fair hair, sometimes widows of fair colouring.

Clubs would indicate a person of medium colour, neither fair nor dark.

Hearts show persons of fair skin, brown hair, blue or grey eyes.

Spades denote those persons who are very dark, black, or dark brown hair, brown eyes.

The characters of those indicated by the cards is usually as follows, but the surrounding cards modify the indications, and should always be most carefully noted.

Spades show melancholy minds, pessimists, a tendency to fits of depression, lacking vitality and capacity for enjoyment.

Clubs denote persons of reliable character, very thorough in all they undertake, methodical, very intelligent. They have a love for understanding the reasons of things. They show energy and a determination to carry anything through they once take up.

Diamonds indicate those full of vitality, sense of humour, vivacity, light-heartedness, much capacity for enjoyment, love of pleasure; these people are usually magnetic, and attract many to them. They sometimes have a tendency to be fickle and uncertain.

Hearts denote people of sympathetic and understanding minds, genial, home-loving, pliable, impressionable. They usually have natures easily led, are fond of entertaining, and possess a gift for being host or hostess.

Those who are not gifted with strong clairvoyance should mark all the cards which lie the same way — such as eights, nines and tens of each suit, as the meanings of

THE PACK

the cards are quite different when reversed.

Knaves often show the thoughts of the kings and queens of the same suit, but they have various other meanings also. All depends upon their position, and how they come up in the counting. Sometimes the knave of clubs will represent a schoolboy or a student, the knave of diamonds a cadet, or a very youthful soldier, or a messenger, telegraph boy, or postman. The knave of hearts shows a lover, a husband, or a very dear friend, the closest friend the consultant has. The knave of spades shows an enemy, or an errand boy.

The significance of the pack of thirty-two cards should be thoroughly mastered before attempting anything further. There is much to remember, and it is most necessary to have it all accurately fixed in the mind before trying to " tell a fortune," except of course your own fortune, which is quite the most satisfactory way of practising and becoming accustomed to the look of the various combinations.

CLUBS

RIGHT.

Ace. Papers, good news, luck, letters, newspaper.

Ten. A short journey or outing, carriage, fortunate and pleasant events.

Nine. Pleasure, legal business.

Eight. A staunch friend, pleasant intercourse and meetings with friends.

Seven. Success, achievement, projects carried out.

REVERSED.

Ace. Disagreeable or bad news, delayed letters.

Ten. An outing near water, sea or river. Sometimes a train journey, with water near the railway.

Nine. Delays, depression, disturbing occurrences, discomforts.

Eight. News, papers, discussion.

Seven. Annoyance about money matters.

HEARTS

RIGHT.

Ace. A house, an affectionate letter.

Ten. Happiness, love, cheerfulness, miti-

THE PACK

gates the meanings of any bad cards to which it may be near.

Nine. The wish card, attainment of desire. things tending to success and pleasure.

Eight. Friends, marriage, invitations, clothes, furniture, affection.

Seven. A small pleasure or gratified wish. Domestics, and domestic affairs.

REVERSED.

Ace. Changes, removals, a home not your own.

Ten. Birth, change, pleasure, enthusiasm.

Nine. Great affection, someone dear to you.

Eight. A tendency to jealousy, sociability.

Seven. Ruffled feelings, a fuss, small agitations.

SPADES

RIGHT.

Ace. A large building, business.

Ten. Water, voyages, distance.

Nine. Loss, failure of plans and hopes, grief.

Eight. Illness, depression, night.

Seven. Change, arrangements, determination.

REVERSED.

Ace. Death, anxiety, annoyance, danger.

Ten. Trouble, illness, bereavement, persons in mourning.

Nine. Grave danger, death, many troubles.

Eight. Gloom, obstacles, sadness, feelings of disappointment, deceit, plotting.

Seven. Upset, disturbance, irritation, accident.

DIAMONDS

RIGHT.

Ace. A present, jewellery, paper money.

Ten. Money.

Nine. Sudden happenings, anger, sharp instruments, firearms, sword. With hearts or clubs or one of its own suit, speed. With spades, grave danger.

Eight. Road, walk, a short outing.

Seven. A brother or sister, child or animal, or inanimate objects.

REVERSED.

Ace. Financial news or letters, money business.

Ten. Engines, fire, electricity.

THE PACK

Nine. Danger, fighting, pain, operation. With spades, death, a coffin.

Eight. Irritability, disagreeables, things going wrong, rudeness.

Seven. A present, a photograph, a parcel.

It is important when laying out the cards to notice carefully those on each side of the one under consideration, whether it be the consultant, the house card, etc. The immediately surrounding cards are of much importance, and should be always carefully considered before coming to a decision. For instance, if the consultant appeared with the eight of spades on her left, the nine of diamonds on her right, with the ten of hearts next to it, you would see that she was in for a sharp illness, with a good deal of pain, but the ten of hearts beyond shows a good recovery and a speedy one. There are many meanings to be learned when several cards of the same value come together. It is important to know these thoroughly. Of course the cartomante will find out various meanings, and will use their significations as the cards become more familiar, in addition to such meanings as may be learned from this book.

FOURS

Four aces. A bad sign, troubles in the home, distress, adversity. Reversed, they show much annoyance, some treachery.

Four kings. Association with those in positions of authority and honour, dignitaries, honours. When reversed they denote undertakings necessitating legal advice.

Four queens. Much talking and discussion sometimes leading to quarrels, gossip. Reversed; carelessness, frivolity, garrulous friends.

Four knaves. Something deceptive and underhand, payments pressed for, difficult to meet. Reversed; a prison, a law court, an asylum.

Four tens. Pleasures, success, that which is undertaken accomplished successfully. Reversed; disagreeable happenings.

Four nines. Fraud, trickery, a robbery. Reversed; love of money.

Four eights. Success and accomplishment

THE PACK 67

of anything taken in hand. Reversed; shows failure and disappointment of hopes.

Four sevens. Young people, children, infants. Reversed; underhand dealings, intrigues.

THREES

Three aces. Shows promotion, rise in position, some pleasing news. Reversed; pleasant meetings.

Three kings. An undertaking successfully carried out. Reversed; you will meet strangers with whom you will become friendly.

Three queens. Social pleasures. Reversed; jealousy, suspicion, scandal.

Three knaves. Plans upset, disputing, irritating occurrences. Reversed; calm indifference.

Three tens. Improving conditions, future happiness, pleasant surroundings. Reversed; trouble, sadness.

Three nines. Delayed arrangements, things going crookedly. Reversed; a tendency to be grasping, selfishness.

Three eights. Cheerfulness, happiness,

marriage. Reversed; dancing, amusements, pleasant outings.

Three sevens. A commotion, disturbed atmosphere, an upset. Reversed; tiresome occurrences, household annoyances, domestic worry.

PAIRS

Two aces. Suggestions and plans, new ideas. Reversed; doubting, indecision, a balancing of " pros and cons."

Two kings. A good friend, friendly and pleasant meetings. Reversed; new ideas.

Two queens. Talk, discussion, friendly advice and conversation. Reversed; disturbance, trouble.

Two knaves. A receipt, a demand, an enquiry. Reversed; a bill, treacherous behaviour.

Two tens. Happy conditions, a pleasant surprise, good luck. Reversed; outings giving much pleasure, meetings with congenial friends.

Two nines. (Red). Something fortunate and giving you pleasure will happen, money. Reversed; speedy happiness through someone dear to you. (Black). A denial, disappointment. Reversed; failure, loss.

Two eights. Plans, pleasure. Reversed; agreements, undertakings.

Two sevens. A suggestion, a proposition. Reversed; ruffled feelings, worry, irritability.

CHAPTER V

DISPLAYING THE CARDS. EXAMPLE CASE NO. 1.

Experience and Practice Necessary in Divining Meanings by Cards. A Thorough Mastery of the Suits and Values of the Cards Essential. The Deal. Keep the Mind Blank. The Shuffle. Its Great Psychological Importance. The Significance of the Subconscious Mind. An Example Case as shown in Plate No. 1. How the Counting should begin. Foretelling the Public News. A Word to Those Who Forget. Events Predicted may be Far Off. Futurity Clear to the Subconsciousness. The Unerring Accuracy of the Cards.

THE foregoing instances of some combinations of the cards will no doubt be found useful, but of course those I have given are only a small selection from the many meanings to be found in the various readings. There is so much in the diverse methods of divination which only experience can teach. Having

DISPLAYING THE CARDS — I

thoroughly mastered the meanings of the suits and the values of the cards, together with the many combined significations belonging to them, the reader passes on to a study of the different ways of laying out the cards.

Taking the thirty-two cards in the left hand, your consultant must shuffle them thoroughly. It is said by some authorities that the cartomante should cut the cards and hand them to the consultant — this seems to me immaterial. Both reader and client should avoid thinking of any special subject, or wish. Keep the mind as far as possible a blank, or think of such ordinary subjects as the weather, flowers, etc. Desire to know the truth, and do not be afraid to know it.

The cards must be not only shuffled in the ordinary way, but some of them should be turned from end to end, quite haphazard, and without any care or thought about method. The turning of the cards in this way is, however, obviously necessary, as the meanings are quite different when reversed. This I have shown in the foregoing pages.

The great psychological importance of the shuffle is obvious. It is from the subconscious mind of the consultant that the knowledge to come is to be transmitted to the cards. This knowledge is conveyed to the consultant through the instrument of the hands, and from there to the cards. What the ordinary mind of the consultant does not know, but desires to know, is thus brought to the surface by the simple process of shuffling. Knowledge is to be expressed and translated by the cards. It is very simple, yet surely very wonderful.

Having shuffled the cards, the consultant cuts them three times, face downwards. The cartomante will then turn up the cards, and interpret the cut, combining the three cards as something greatly occupying the mind of the consultant, or some event near at hand.

For instance, we will suppose that the consultant is the queen of hearts, a married woman. She cuts the king of hearts (having already ascertained that her husband is of her own colouring) the ace of spades and the eight of spades — showing illness,

PLATE I.

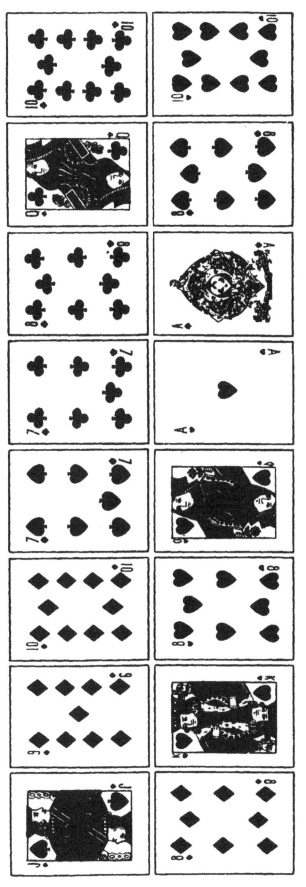

Reproduced by kind permission of Messrs. Charles Goodall & Son, Ltd.

DISPLAYING THE CARDS — I

necessitating her husband going to a nursing home or hospital. The cards are then picked up in the order in which they were cut, 1, 2, 3. Holding them back upwards, they are laid out as follows: — Place each card one by one, face upwards, so that the first eight form a straight line from left to right.

Again from left to right, lay out the cards in the next row of eight, immediately under the first row. Proceed in this way until all the thirty-two cards are placed in front of you in four rows of eight cards. Still supposing the queen of hearts to be the consultant, who is clearly troubled in mind, as shown by the cut, we see that she comes out in the centre of the second row. The eight of hearts between this queen of hearts and her husband shows their bond of affection. On her right is the house card (ace of hearts) and ace of spades, with the seven of clubs, and seven of spades, reversed, at her head. This signifies worry and difficulty as to plans, increased by the fact that the two sevens, reversed, as they touch a money card, ten of diamonds, shows expense has to be considered in the matter of her husband's illness, which is to lead to his going to a nursing home. This latter fact is shown by the ace of spades and eight of spades touching. The eight of clubs (reversed) and queen of clubs, touching the cards representing the nursing home, shows the talk and arrangements being made with a nurse. The ten of hearts and ten of clubs, beyond and above the nursing home, indicate a delightful change after the illness, and complete recovery.

It will be seen that the king of hearts is touched by the nine of diamonds, knave of spades, and eight of diamonds, showing the arrival of the doctor. Also, as the nine of diamonds, eight of diamonds, ten of diamonds, reversed, shows a motor car, and there are obvious signs of illness and accident, it is known that the king of hearts has met with an accident in a motor car though not a serious one.

The counting should begin with the consultant, the queen of hearts, that card counting as the first. Then pass on to the third, which is to be considered in connec-

DISPLAYING THE CARDS — I

tion with the two preceding cards, and the one next to it. From the third card count on to the seventh, which must be considered with those touching it. Proceed similarly from the seventh to the ninth, and from that to the thirteenth. From the thirteenth counting begins again, number one being the card next to the thirteenth. The cards should be linked up in each count, as the third and the seventh, the seventh and the ninth, the ninth and the thirteenth, and so on all through the reading.

The consultant in this case counts first to the king of hearts (third card), the eight of hearts being the connecting card — one of affection, marriage. The third card being the king of hearts counts to the seventh card, the ten of diamonds, touched by the nine of diamonds, seven of spades, reversed, with eight of diamonds below, gives evidence of the cause of the illness, necessitating the summoning of the doctor, shown by the knave of spades and nine of diamonds.

As the queen of hearts counts to the seventh card, touched as it is by the nine of diamonds, which in turn touches the eight of diamonds, and there being no diamond ace to show a railway journey, we see that she will go with her husband in a car to the nursing home. The ninth card shows the state of the consultant's mind, bearing out the theory that what is uppermost in the subconsciousness of the one who shuffles the cards will be shown in the cut. The thirteenth card, ten of hearts, reversed, shows that although at the present time she is worried and upset over this illness, with the changes it involves things will improve before long and there will be a pleasant ending and happiness.

Counting on from the eight of spades as one, to the third card, the ace of hearts we see indication of trouble at the house and the plans arranged for taking one of the inmates to a nursing home. As the seventh card is the eight of diamonds, the ninth and the thirteenth, the nine of diamonds and eight of clubs reversed, we know that a telegram is despatched by bicycle to the queen of clubs touching the ace of spades and eight of spades, therefore the matron or sister of the nursing home.

DISPLAYING THE CARDS — I 77

As only two rows are shown, the counting has gone round again to the top line; usually it would proceed downwards, taking each row one after the other, although the counting may be in any direction from any point; but it is certainly advisable to count in the systematic way explained first of all.

This should always begin with the consultant, the ace of hearts for the home, the ace of clubs for letters, the nine of hearts for the wish.

As a means of gaining further information from the display, it is a good plan to count from each of these cards up and down the rows of four, as well as from side to side.

This secondary counting is best done in sevens, nines and thirteens only, omitting the special counting in threes.

It is useful sometimes to ask consultants if there is any one particular court card from which they would like a counting. There may be someone in whom they are specially interested. This plan is generally found to be satisfactory in its results.

As an illustration, in the cards displayed

in the plate, a count from the king of hearts will show his fate quite clearly, and how it came about. Having counted in every direction along each row from the consultant, ace of hearts, ace of clubs, nine of hearts, then up and down each row, proceed to take up the cards as follows: —

First take the card of the first row and the last card of the bottom row, bring them together and read their combined meaning. Do likewise with the second card of the top row and the last card but one of the fourth row. Continue thus, row by row, until the whole pack is exhausted, in each case reading the two cards thus brought together to form a combined reading.

Before beginning to count, it is important to take special notice of the cards touching the consultant, house card, and wish card, as this gives a general indication of the desires and conditions surrounding your client. It will often be found in laying out the cards for some persons, that very few events of definite interest seem visible. This must be so if the consultant's life is made up of

DISPLAYING THE CARDS — I 79

small affairs and diversions, and she seeks information from the cards only as an interlude from "the daily round, the common task." In such cases the seer must make the most of such trivial events and incidents, remembering that they are interesting to the consultant. The ace of clubs in every case yields information which is sure to be of some importance to the consultant. Every life is not brimful of violent contrasts, sorrow and joy, tragedy and comedy.

From the position of the ace of clubs, in connection with the court cards to which it may count, it is sometimes difficult to be sure if news or a letter is coming to the consultant, or if it is only a correspondence less personal, of which she will be told. It will usually be found, however, that the eight of clubs reversed, intervening between the letter card and the card of the significators, is an indication that the news in the letter will concern the consultant, and there will be talk and discussion over the matter. The ace of clubs counting to several court cards, and the eight of hearts show an invitation to a party.

If the consultant faces the ace of clubs, the letters are coming to her from the various court cards to which it counts.

If the consultant's card has its back to the ace of clubs, she has sent the letters to the various people indicated by the court cards to which it counts.

Do not forget that events recorded in the newspapers are quite likely to appear, such as a railway strike, ten of spades reversed, ten of diamonds, reversed, ace of spades with knave of spades and knave of clubs touching.

A murder may be foretold. In this case the cards would probably fall with several spade cards together, with nine of diamonds reversed, ace of spades reversed, with king of spades and knave of spades touching. The reading of the cards is not limited to purely personal affairs.

Of course, everything depends upon the general indication of the cards, and how the various countings come as a whole. It is certainly necessary for the seer to warn those consulting the cards not to be too ready to attach events to certain people

DISPLAYING THE CARDS — I

whom they consider are represented by the court cards.

In many cases it is quite clear that certain persons are indicated. It often happens that those for whom the cards are being read are too hasty in identifying persons who seem to be indicated in the cards, and mistakes are made. There may be much unnecessary anxiety, or hopes may be raised only to be proved false. In any case, warn your consultant to keep an open mind as to identification, except of course where it is quite obvious that the court card is pointing to a certain person.

When counting from each of the four cards already specified as the significator, house, news, and wish cards, and the count leads you to a court card, pause at that point and consider its surroundings. They will often disclose the identity of the person as represented by the court card. If it be a king, the profession is often to be seen by the cards touching, as the king of spades, ace of spades — a clergyman. If a queen, if she is married, a widow, someone in mourning and so on.

It is of great value to those who are consulting the cards to hear news of their friends, or perhaps far-off relatives. When such can be readily recognised by the consultant, it is desirable to give as much detail about them as possible. It is often useful, when such information is particularly desired, to count from the court card representing that person. In this case, count in nines and thirteens only, having first studied the immediate surroundings of the card under consideration.

There is an old saying, " What falls on the floor comes to the door." It is a very remarkable fact that, whenever a court card leaps out of the pack during the shuffle and falls to the ground, a person of that colouring invariably does " Come to the door." I have never known it fail. I have seen it happen when the plain cards " fall to the floor," such as the nine of spades, or the wish card (nine of hearts), or a money card. This, however, cannot be laid down as a certainty as in the case of court cards. It is a small fact, but surely a most interesting one! At any rate it is worth while to

DISPLAYING THE CARDS — I

tell the consultant, if such a falling of the court cards take place, that the person indicated by the fallen card is likely to be coming to see her.

There are some people who are most attentive whilst having their cards read, but who forget almost immediately after what has been told them. All they recollect are just those incidents closely concerning them individually. They are then apt to decide that the cards are "all wrong," whereas, it is quite as likely that the memory of the consultant is "all wrong." Impress on the mind of each consultor of the cards that events predicted may be far off, and if they are worth hearing they are worth remembering.

I recently heard the whole subject of card-reading summed up and dismissed by one who had ventured to have her fortune told. She remarked, "Oh! my experience of card-reading is that you are merely told you will meet a fair man, or a dark man!"

Here is a case where condemnation of the whole faculty of card-reading is entirely the result of faulty memory. Who can suppose for one moment that the cards afforded no more information than that which she gave as being the sum total of her experience of card-reading? The cards are truth itself, as indeed they must be, so far as the knowledge of coming events is concerned. Futurity is clear to the subconsciousness, of which the cards are the reflection; and when events are predicted and statements made that have no foundation, the fault lies with the diviner, not in the power of the cards. Their unerring truth is sometimes almost provoking, if I may so express it.

I have tried often to foresee something happening for myself, something of much importance and particularly desirable. I have spread the cards, and studied them and they have plainly shown that such an event will not come about as I have wished it to do. Again and again I have felt extremely annoyed with the cards, because they will not show me that which I so much desired to see! I have done this many times and for various reasons, but I have never once found that they can be coerced into

DISPLAYING THE CARDS — I

doing what the consultant may wish them to do. The desires of the ordinary consciousness have no power against the clear sight and judgment of the subconscious mind's revealing. Attempts at coercion should be tried only from an experimental point of view. It is the greatest possible mistake to force the cards in any way. It can only end in failure. The more simple, natural, and detached the attitude towards them the better.

CHAPTER VI

EXAMPLE CASES Nos. II AND III

A Second Example of the Same Method. See Plate No. 2. "The Star of Fortune." Equally Efficacious When the Consultant is Absent. The Representative Card of the Significator Placed in the Centre. The Order in Which the Cards are Dealt, as Shown in the Plate. A Happy Example of the "Star of Fortune."

There are some people for whom the cards seem to give a much clearer rendering when done by a different method than that which the cartomante may be in the habit of using. It is a curious fact that individuality should sometimes so affect the divination as to make it easier in one way than in another, but so it is; therefore, when this is found to be the case try a different method. For that reason alone it is well worth while to

PLATE II.

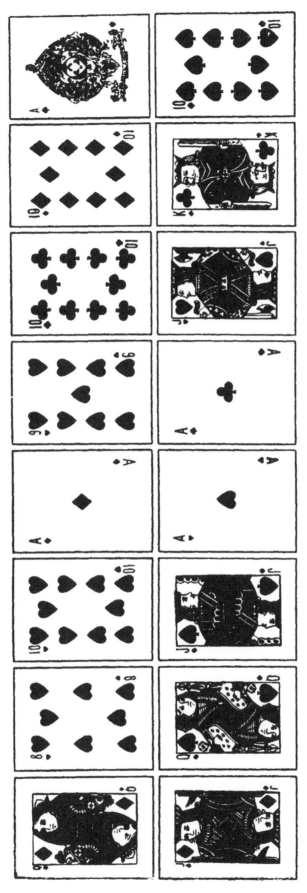

Reproduced by kind permission of Messrs. Charles Goodall & Son, Ltd

DISPLAYING THE CARDS—II & III

learn the different examples of displaying the cards given in this book, though personally I have always found that the method already given works well for everyone. It is comprehensive and full of possibilities, owing to its variety of countings. As the student of the cards becomes proficient, it will be found that the cards and their combined meanings become clearer, and more easily recognised. Many events are sure to be symbolised other than those learned from a book. It may be helpful to give a second illustration of the cards done by the same method as before.

We will now take the case of a very fair girl, the queen of diamonds, and see briefly how the cards show for her an engagement, and a happy marriage.

In this display the significator, the queen of diamonds, is seen at the top of the first row of cards, with promise of coming happiness through a man whom she already knows. He is in the row beneath her — the king of clubs — and it is clearly shown that he is a sailor on a destroyer or battleship, and that through his ability and success in all he undertakes (three tens) he will have something awaiting him of a most fortunate nature. A real piece of good luck. This good news he hurriedly despatches in a letter to the queen of diamonds, who is eagerly hoping for it, as certainly she will be with three aces, and the nine and ten of hearts touching them. This lucky success and promotion make money conditions much easier, and enable the king of clubs to make an offer of marriage to the queen of diamonds, which is obviously accepted.

Below the queen of diamonds is the queen of spades and her knave on one side, and the knave of diamonds on the other. This shows a woman who is a widow, an unpleasant person with a dangerous tongue. She has been a menace and an obstacle to the queen of diamonds; and her thoughts, shown by the spade knave, are turning towards the affairs of the queen of diamonds. She knows of the engagement and would like to interfere with it if she could.

Now a court card with a knave each side of it usually represents a person with whom it is very necessary to be on your guard.

DISPLAYING THE CARDS—II & III

Luckily in this case there is no chance of this woman doing actual mischief. The good cards surrounding the queen of diamonds secure her against any interference with her happiness. As will be seen the thoughts of the queen of diamonds (knave of diamonds) have been, perhaps, unconsciously, hovering about this woman, whom she knows to be undesirable. But she has nothing to fear.

It will be seen in counting from the queen of diamonds, which is touching the eight of hearts and ten of hearts, that the consultant is very shortly to become engaged and married. The third card linked up to the seventh card, the ten of diamonds, tells us that she will take a railway journey. The ninth card being the ten of spades, which is touching its ace, shows that her destination is far distant, and that it is by water as shown by the ten of spades, this card touching the ace, and the ten of diamonds shows that it is a place of battleships. We should therefore be safe in predicting a seaside place with a naval station. The king of clubs touching these three cards, with the knave of hearts beside him, show his identity as the man whom she is going to meet at the journey's end. The thirteenth card, the ace of hearts (reversed), shows the house to which the change takes her.

It will be seen in counting from the thirteenth card, and taking the next card as one (knave of spades) that we come to the knave of diamonds, showing the thoughts of the queen, which are now full of the coming happiness she has wished for. The fortunate turn events have taken brings her to the meeting with the king of clubs, and the arrangements for their marriage, which he has already spoken of in a letter, and which owing to his promotion are now possible.

THE STAR OF FORTUNE

It is useful sometimes to have a system of reading the cards which can be done quite satisfactorily for a particular person without that person being present. It is also found very interesting for certain consultants who may wish for information about someone in whom they are specially interested.

Plate III.

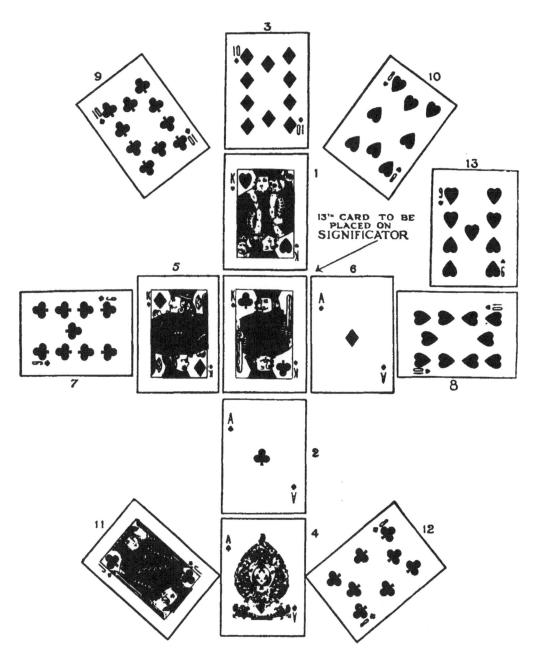

Reproduced by kind permission of Messrs. Charles Goodall & Son, Ltd.

DISPLAYING THE CARDS — II & III

It is not necessary for the consultant to show to the seer the court card which they take to represent the person about whom they desire information. Simply let it be placed face downwards on the table, the consultant shuffles as usual, but in this case the mind must be resolutely fixed on the person about whom the knowledge is desired. The consultant should be warned of this before the shuffling of the cards begins, and nothing must be permitted to disturb the concentration. The need for this concentration can be easily explained. When special information is being sought with regard to someone, other than the consultant, and when the seeker of that information is handling the cards and has, as it were, to represent that individual and make their minds one, then thought-concentration upon this absent person is most necessary.

When the reading of this " Star of Fortune " is for the consultant, first take the representative card for the significator, and place it on the table, face upwards. The remaining thirty-one cards are then shuffled and as far as possible the mind kept blank. Having thoroughly shuffled the cards and cut in the usual way into three packs, take note of the " cut " and interpret it. Remember that a good " cut " will mitigate an ominous-looking display of cards, just as a bad " cut " (such as the nine of spades, eight of spades and a diamond) will add to the gloom of an unpromising lay out of the cards.

Take up the cards in the order in which they were cut — 1, 2, 3. At the head of the significator deal the first card. The second at the feet. The third at the head. The fourth at the feet. The fifth on the left. The sixth on the right. The seventh on the left. The eighth on the right. The ninth above, and on the left of the significator. The tenth above, and on the right of the significator. The eleventh below, and on the left of the significator. The twelfth below, and on the right of the significator. The thirteenth card is to be placed on the significator, as seen in the plate.

If the nine of hearts, or ten of hearts, comes out as the thirteenth card, it is a good

DISPLAYING THE CARDS — II & III

omen, but if the nine of spades touches the significator, it spoils its meaning, and cherished hopes will have to be abandoned. Three nines appearing shows a tedious waiting, things going crookedly. If the nine of spades is one of the three, it is a rather hopeless outlook for plans. Four kings touching the significator, supposing it to be a queen, would be a good sign, those in whom she is most interested attaining to a position of power and honour. It is a pleasing sign when the significator is crowned with good cards, such as hearts, or hearts and clubs. Hope may then be entertained that the ambitions will be realised, but if spades and diamonds, or all spades are at the head of the significator, it is not a promising outlook.

It should be borne in mind that diamond cards must always be regarded in relation to the cards they touch. They are very good with hearts and clubs, but extremely bad with spades. Even if the significator has bad cards at her feet, good cards at her head will show troubles that she has gone through, the worst of them being over. It is a good outlook for the future. The future prospects, and the past conditions which influence the present, may be judged at once by the general aspect of the cards.

This short method of divination is very useful when information is needed on any special subject, such, for instance as the result of any necessary project, in business undertakings, journeys, public or private affairs; their advantages, or disadvantages. This can be done with any appropriate card being placed in the centre as the significator, such as the

Ace of clubs with regard to letters, papers, news.

Ace of diamonds with regard to money matters.

Ace of hearts for the house.

I have explained in the beginning of this chapter how information may be acquired by this method of doing the cards, even when the consultant is not present, but has merely sent a deputy.

An example of this method of doing the cards is shown on Plate III. The king of clubs is the significator, evidently a most successful and prosperous man. Everything seems to be going exactly as he wishes it. Evidence of this lies in each direction. He is touched by kings, diamonds and clubs. The thirteenth card is the nine of hearts, the wish card, what could be better? His thoughts have been centered on news from a publisher's office, shown by the ace of clubs touching ace of spades, eight of clubs (reversed) knave of clubs. Satisfactory news from this direction will mean very much to him. There are no apparent obstacles in this fortunate man's path. The cards on the left are full of success and fortunate business, which he seems to have transacted to a great extent with a friend, who has a great regard for the significator. This is shown by the eight of hearts touching the king of hearts. The cards at the head of the significator speak of the monetary success of his project. He appears to have a most flourishing career before him. The financial news is again shown by the eight of clubs (reversed) and the ace of diamonds. That it is good news is plainly seen again by the ten of hearts being in connection with both these cards. The three aces show the good news coming for him. The eight of hearts and ace of diamonds in connection with the ten of diamonds, show an invitation to go on a journey, evidently one much to his taste, and with the eight of hearts, ace of diamonds, ten of diamonds and ten of hearts in connection, we may safely conclude the journey leads to additional happiness for him. An engagement and wedding are shown. The wish card being the thirteenth card shows the realisation of his desires.

CHAPTER VII

TWO OTHER METHODS

A Method of Laying Out the Cards Without a Cut. "The Month's Events." Methods of Dealing as Shown in Diagram. The Significator in the Centre. A Further Method. Still Another Method. "The Circle of Ten" (see diagram). A Fortunate Example Explained.

ANOTHER method of laying out the cards may be interesting and useful. It is simple, and will be found to give satisfactory results for such events and conditions as may be developing within a few weeks. This setting-out of the cards may be tried after the general aspect for the consultant has been given by the method I first described. It is a mistake to tell those seeking information through the cards that this method

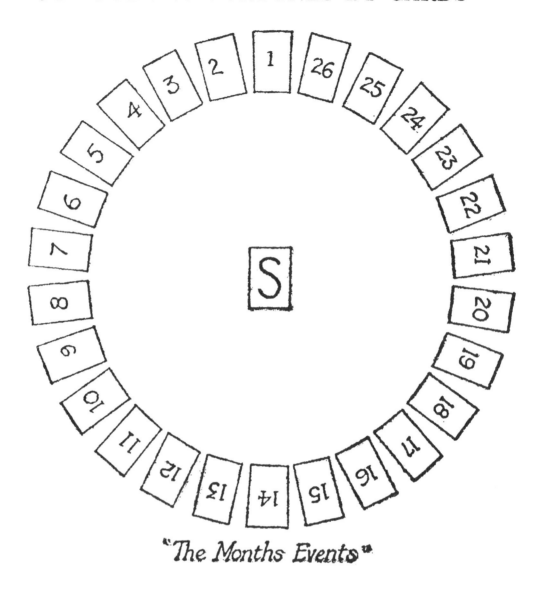

"The Months Events"

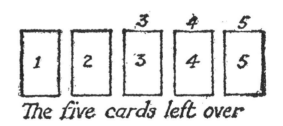

The five cards left over

TWO OTHER METHODS 99

predicts " for the week." As a matter of fact very often events shown do not materialise for several weeks. If the predictions are good, the delay leads to a feeling of disappointment if not of repudiation of the cards. If the prediction is of misfortune and it tarries, then the feeling of relief is too much mingled with apprehension to be enviable. I find it wiser to say that this method foretells events coming within a month. So we will call it " The Month's Events."

First place the significator in the centre. Give the remaining thirty-one cards to the consultant to shuffle. There is no " cut " in this way of laying out the cards. After the shuffle the cartomante takes the pack and places the two top cards side by side, face upwards, over the significator. The first card she puts at the head, the second on the left of it, as shown in the diagram, position No. 2. The third card is then put aside. Continue doing this, each time putting the two top cards on the left hand in the circle round the significator and the third card aside, until two cards only are left in the hand. Then pick up those put aside, and give them to the consultant to shuffle once more. After this repeat the process as before, laying down the first two cards, and putting the third aside until all the cards are used, and a circle of twenty-six cards is formed round the significator.

There will now be five cards left over. Put these aside until the circle has been read. The counting of the twenty-six cards begins from the card immediately over the significator (see diagram card No. 1) to the third card on the left of it. Next from the third to the seventh, and from that card to the ninth and thirteenth. Each one forming a link till the card from which the counting began is reached once more. Then count in exactly the same way from the card next to the one from which the count was begun (No. 1 card). Card No. 2 will now be the one to start from — counting it as No. 1, continuing it in threes, sevens, nines, and thirteens as before. So continue until all the cards have been in turn the first card for a round of counting. The house card, the ace of clubs for news and letters, the

TWO OTHER METHODS 101

wish card, may be similarly dealt with if desired.

The counting should begin from left to right, as shown in the numbered diagram. The cards surrounding the ace of hearts, the ace of clubs and the wish card should be noticed. Good cards round these are a hopeful sign. The cards immediately above the significator are of course most important. If the ten of hearts, or nine of hearts should be in this position it is very encouraging. The card at the foot is also important if it is a court card. It denotes the influence of someone much in the life of the consultant. Any court cards, as well as the others mentioned that may come out in the circle of twenty-six may be counted from, if the consultant wishes.

Now as to how the cards should be taken up. This is done in pairs, each pair forming a separate reading. Begin with the card immediately over the significator (card No. 1) and the card at the foot (card No. 13). Then lift the card next on the left (No. 2 card) with its equivalent card below (No. 12), until all the cards on the left side are paired.

102 TELLING FORTUNES BY CARDS

Begin again in exactly the same way on the right side of the circle. Card No. 26 with No. 14, and so on, until the pairing is complete, with the exception of No. 7 leaving No. 20 to be paired with No. 7 on opposite side. Lastly take up the five cards left over from the circle of twenty-six. Having given them to the consultant to shuffle, place them on the table again in a row — 1, 2, 3, 4, 5. The cartomante then reads them thus: 1, 2, 3 — 3, 4, 5. The third card being the connecting link is used twice in counting. These five cards will indicate a condition, or happening, it may be only a triviality, which is near at hand for the consultant.

With some people one way of divination seems to afford a clearer result than another. I therefore give a further method.

Shuffle the thirty-two cards, cut into three packs and interpret the cut. The cards are then taken up in the order in which they were cut. This is always most important, for if the packs were not taken up in their right order, the whole reading would be thrown out. Deal the cards into eight

TWO OTHER METHODS 103

packs, four cards in each. The dealing is done by putting one card to each pack, from the first card dealt to the eighth — 1, 2, 3, 4, 5, 6, 7, 8, then beginning at the first pack again, until the thirty-two cards are used.

Next ask the consultant to choose one of the packs to represent: —

1. Yourself.
2. Your wish.
3. Your greatest friend.
4. The house.
5. Things to do.
6. Things to avoid.
7. Things which must come.
8. Your hope of success.

Having chosen each pack to represent these eight inquiries, place them in the order in which they are given.

No. 1. For yourself.
No. 2. For your wish.
No. 3. For your greatest friend.
No. 4. For the house.
No. 5. For things to do.
No. 6. For things to avoid.

No. 7. For things which must come.
No. 8. For your hope of success.

Each pack of four is taken up separately and read in three pairs, 1 and 2, 2 and 3, 3 and 4. Deal with each pack of four in this way, the packs being interpreted with regard to their representative positions. For instance, suppose the four cards signifying your wish are the four cards: — Nine of hearts, ace of clubs, ace of diamonds, eight of hearts. This shows that your wish will undoubtedly be gratified, and the news you hope for is coming, together with a letter of plans, most pleasant ones, also an invitation, bringing you that which you desire. Thus you go through the whole of the eight packs in order. Often in this way of laying out the cards the events happen in about a week, but constantly the predictions are for days much further off. Therefore it seems best not to specify too definitely the distance of time belonging to the method of prognostication.

Still another method of doing the cards is simple and yet uses the whole pack. It

TWO OTHER METHODS

has many readings to be interpreted, and will be found useful. This way is called

THE CIRCLE OF TEN

1. For yourself.
2. For your home.
3. For your friends.
4. Your endeavours.
5. Your money affairs.
6. Your pleasures.
7. Your possible calamities.
8. Your present conditions.
9. Your future.
10. Your wish.

First take from the pack the card representing the consultant. Then let the cards be shuffled, or at any rate handled for a few minutes. The cartomante holds the pack of thirty-one loosely in the hand, while the consultant draws three cards.

These three cards are placed face downwards in position No. 1 (see diagram). The next draw of three is placed in position No. 2, representing the home. In each case of this drawing of three cards, place them in the order in which they are drawn and in

106 TELLING FORTUNES BY CARDS

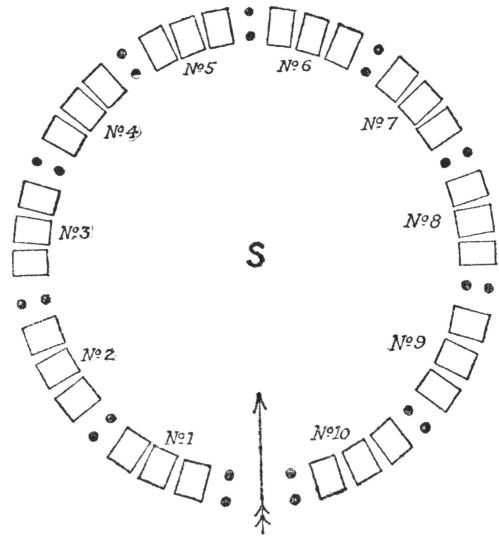

"The Circle of Ten"

TWO OTHER METHODS 107

the position for which they are intended. Keep strictly to the order in which the significations are given. The drawing may be done in single cards, so long as they are placed in a pack of three before the next drawing, or they may be withdrawn in a pack of three if preferred. It is a matter of personal taste and instinct, and will not interfere with the ultimate reading of the circle — so long as each position represented by three cards is not altered. The consultant should be told, before each drawing of three cards, the signification of its position, so that the choice of the three cards, which may be drawn haphazard from any part of the pack, may be deliberate.

The thirty-second card left over from this dealing into packs of three is placed on the significator. It is a card of importance. If it is a court card, it shows a person who has, or will have, much influence in the life of the significator. Ten of hearts, ace of clubs, or nine of hearts, would each of them be good cards to come out as the thirty-first card. Even if the circle has come out well in the reading, if the nine of spades comes on the significator as the thirty-first card, it will mar the prognostication greatly, showing much disappointment and delay. It should be remembered, in reading these packs, that the three cards are read with the second card as the connecting link between the two others. We will take some examples of this.

The king of diamonds is the significator. The first three cards drawn for himself are:— Ten of diamonds, eight of hearts, queen of spades, showing a rich widow, who is evidently someone of influence in his life as she appears in that position. She is probably of financial use to him also. The next three, representing his home — eight of spades, ace of clubs, ace of diamonds, show a letter mentioning a slight illness of a friend or relative, also a cheque or paper money sent through the post, and a letter of plans, pleasant ones, though it will cost money to carry them through.

The third pack representing his friends, shows the seven of clubs, nine of spades, queen of diamonds. The consultant not being a married man, we conclude the fair

TWO OTHER METHODS 109

woman in this pack is a great friend, and he is worried and sad about her. She is evidently in great trouble, as the nine of spades and seven of clubs are reversed. The fourth pack shows us what his endeavours have been and will be. Here we have the knave of hearts, ten of spades (reversed) and king of spades. These cards seem to continue the explanation of the queen of diamonds and her troubles. Here is the knave of hearts to show she is the greatest friend of the consultant, but there is a complete separation at present. Spades are hedging her in, there is illness, distance, and also a formidable obstacle in the king of spades, who is the last card in the pack.

Evidently the endeavours of the king of diamonds to smooth things out and lessen the troubles of this fair woman are of no avail at present, but if good cards come out in the last pack, the three cards representing the wish, we shall know that in the end his attempts to aid her have attained success.

The fifth pack is indicative of money affairs. From the three cards shown: Ace of hearts, nine of diamonds, knave of clubs, these appear to be eminently satisfactory. Clubs and diamonds in a pack representative of money are of course very good, showing success and prosperity. It is certain that there is no financial worry attached. The sixth pack indicates pleasures. Here is the eight of diamonds, nine of clubs, ace of spades, showing there will be pleasure at a concert or theatre. The distance to this theatre, or concert hall, is evidently not great — the eight of diamonds showing this, and that there will be a walk to the theatre or concert.

The seventh pack shows possible calamities that may befall him. In this pack there are the king and queen of clubs and seven of spades. There does not seem to be anything very serious, but evidently the change (seven of spades) that comes with this couple does mean something, at any rate vexing, to the consultant, otherwise these cards would not have fallen in the seventh position. The pending change for that couple evidently affects the king of diamonds in some uncomfortable way, but most certainly it is a calamity of a mild nature.

TWO OTHER METHODS 111

The eighth pack is the present. The first card in this pack is the seven of diamonds (reversed), ace of spades, knave of spades, showing that there is some monetary affair over which there is business with a bank manager. As was seen in the pack representing the money affairs, all seems well in that direction. The ninth pack is representative of the future, which looks very promising of happiness and good fortune, as the king and queen of hearts appear, together with the ten of clubs. The king and queen in this case show happiness coming through a great affection which is mutual — and the ten of clubs shows the fortunate position attending the king of diamonds.

The tenth and last pack brings us to the wish. Here is the knave of diamonds, eight of clubs (reversed), nine of hearts. It is most fortunate to find the nine of hearts (wish card) in the tenth position. Most surely he will have his wish. No doubt that which he has been endeavouring to accomplish, and in which he has been hindered by adverse circumstances, as we saw in the fourth pack, will soon come about. The news, as shown by the reversed eight of clubs next to the wish card, shows the desired news certainly coming. His thoughts are centered round this wish of his, as seen by the knave of diamonds. If any additional evidence is needed, it is seen in the ten of hearts, being the thirty-first card on the significator which is eminently satisfactory.

I have given an example of a fortunate circle, for though the consultant's greatest friend is in a sorry case for the present, obviously that cloud passes, otherwise the packs indicating the future and his wish and the thirty-first card would not be so good, or so indicative of happiness.

I would strongly recommend this method of doing the cards. The reading in packs of three in accordance with their relative positions is simple, and the position packs give much information, even though the cards are limited to three only.

CHAPTER VIII

THE FOUR FANS

A Short Method of Dealing the Cards, called "The Four Fans" (see diagram). A Popular Method and a Quick Means of Prediction. How to do the Counting. Examples of the First, Second, Third, and Fourth Fans. A Capital Method for a Cartomante to Use When Demonstrating and Reading at a Party.

ANOTHER short method of doing the cards will no doubt be appreciated, as it is simple, very easy to remember, and useful when a short way of reading is needed. It will probably be found a popular method, as all the cards are used, and yet it is a quick means of prediction. It is called "The Four Fans."

The consultant first shuffles the cards

for a few minutes, and hands them to the seer, who holds them face downwards, loosely in the hand, while the consultant draws eight cards at random from any part of the pack. The consultant should be told before the drawing begins, that the eight cards may be drawn separately, or if preferred two or more may be drawn together till the eight cards are all withdrawn from the pack. This should be a matter of instinctive choice on the part of the consultant.

The cards are placed as drawn, face upwards on the left (position No. 1 in diagram), in the shape of a fan. Be careful to put the cards down on the table in the exact order in which they were drawn. This is most important. Then eight more cards are drawn in the same way, and placed on the left hand above the No. 1 position, as shown in the diagram. Again draw eight cards. These are placed in the same way (position No. 3) on the right, opposite the top pack on the left. Lastly, the remaining eight cards are drawn and placed opposite the lower fan on the left side. Each fan is then read in accordance with its respective positions.

THE FOUR FANS 115

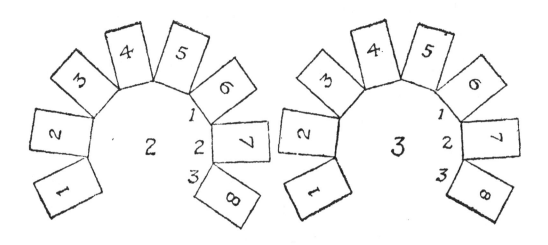

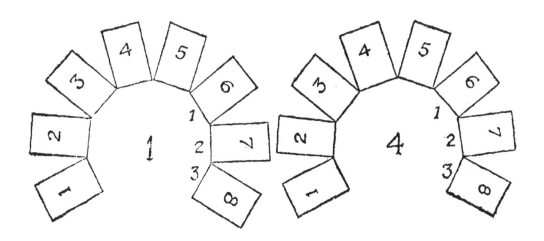

"The Four Fans"

Position No. 1. Represents "That you will gain."

Position No. 2. Represents "That you will lose."

Position No. 3. Represents "That you may have."

Position No. 4. Represents "That you would choose."

The counting is done in four pairs, using the third card of the fan each time as the first card for the next count.

To make the last count of the three cards at the end of the fan complete, the sixth card of the fan is used as No. 1 card, irrespective of the fact that the card next to it would come as No. 3, after the third counting. Taking the last count of the packs in this way, No. 6 card is now No. 1 card for the final counting in each fan — as shown in the diagram, and No. 6 card is marked as No. 1, on the opposite side. The counting in each case begins at the left of the fan, as will be seen in the diagram, with No. 1 card marked in its right position.

The first fan to be read will be No. 1. An example of this method may be helpful.

THE FOUR FANS

For instance, No. 1 pack representing "That you will gain," has — seven of spades, ten of hearts, ace of clubs (reversed), ten of clubs, ten of spades, king of spades, ace of hearts. The ace of clubs being reversed, the news about the change which is coming will be less pleasant than it would otherwise have been, but the benefit will certainly outdo any disadvantages, as the ten of hearts is the centre card. The change will certainly be a gain for you.

The ace of clubs again as No. 1 card this time with ten of clubs, ten of spades shows a letter from abroad. As the ace is reversed it shows delay in the arrival of the letter, and the news is not so satisfactory as if the ace had been the right way up.

The ten of spades as No. 1 card this time, with ace of spades and king of spades, shows a yachtsman, through whom there is pleasure. As the No. 1 card is the next count of three with the ace of spades and ace of hearts, it indicates this yachtsman is evidently coming to the house. There are plans connected with him which will no doubt be very pleasant.

The next position (No. 2 fan) represents "That you will lose." For this fan we have: — Eight of diamonds, seven of diamonds (reversed), seven of hearts, eight of spades, queen of clubs, seven of clubs (reversed), queen of spades, eight of hearts.

Counting from No. 1 card, the eight of diamonds, the reversed seven of diamonds, and seven of hearts, we find that taken in connection with the position of these cards something valued, probably a present, has been lost while out of doors. The seven of hearts is the next card from which to count. This touching the eight of spades shows loss of a domestic. Card No. 3 shows her to be the queen of clubs, and evidently, taken in connection with the next count, she is worried about illness of a woman, the queen of spades, who is a widow, as shown by the last two cards of the fan. It is clear that the loss of this domestic is caused through the illness of this widow, who is probably her mother, and her illness necessitates the maid's departure.

Position No. 3 stands for "That you may have." In this fan is shown the nine of

THE FOUR FANS

clubs, knave of spades, eight of clubs (reversed), nine of spades, king of clubs, ace of diamonds, king of diamonds, queen of diamonds. In the first count of three we have a lawyer, and talk and papers connected with legal business. "What you may have," appears to be disappointing or troublesome news, as, in the next count of three there is the nine of spades touching the king of clubs, who is evidently the man of business discussing the money affairs with the lawyer.

The king of clubs, as the first card in the second count of three, counts to the king of diamonds, the ace of diamonds is between them. As the diamonds and clubs are touching, with two kings it shows that affairs will turn out better than they appeared at the beginning of the fan, and ending as it does with all diamond court cards it is most encouraging.

The last fan of cards indicates "That which would be your choice." If the wish card, unaccompanied by spades, should come in the eight cards, it would mean "that you would choose" will be that which you shall have. The first three cards in this fan are the nine of diamonds, and king and queen of hearts, showing something most pleasing with regard to a fair couple, an affair which is rapidly developing.

The queen of hearts counting as No. 1 card in the second count of three, shows very good news with regard to money matters. Ten of diamonds with the knave of clubs as the centre card, tells of the satisfactory news. The ten of diamonds next, as the No. 1 card in the last count of three, with the knave of hearts, and nine of hearts, is a most promising and hopeful ending.

There are not only signs of prosperity, but of happy affection and wished for conditions connected with the dearest friend of the consultant. The cards falling as in this example of " That you will choose " is singularly fortunate. There could be no doubt in this case that all would go well for those for whom the cards were so auspicious.

Of course it cannot invariably happen that each one has such undoubted good luck, but it is eminently satisfactory for the reader

THE FOUR FANS 121

of the cards to be the interpreter of unclouded happiness and success. It can scarcely give more pleasure to the consultant than to the humble translator of the cards, when such delightful conditions are foreshown. It is easy to proclaim that which you know will be extremely pleasant to hear. It is horribly hard even to hint at the opposite conditions of gloom and greyness.

This method of reading the cards in packs of eight divided into three counts of three in each fan, read in relation to their respective positions gives a good deal of information without much time being spent on the reading. It would be found suitable if the cartomante is called upon to read the cards of several people, let us say at a party, or on any occasion when comparatively little time can be spent upon each individual.

As a method for those who wish the cards consulted very often, it is most useful, though there are several other ways suitable for a time limit reading such as " The Circle of Ten."

CHAPTER IX

YOUR LIFE

Cards Drawn and Not Dealt. Placed as Shown in Diagram. The Three Positions. Methods of Reading and Interpretation. Taking Up in Pairs. "The Four Knaves." A Method in Which These are Used as Significators Representing the Twelve Months of the Year. The Four Positions as Shown in Diagram. Methods of Dealing. The Seventh Card a Lucky Number Used for Seventh Day of the Week. The Counting of the Cards in the Four Positions. Days we Consider Lucky or Unlucky. Groups in Which a Birthday Falls. A Short and Simple Method. "Things of To-day, To-morrow, Joy or Sorrow."

It is always useful for a cartomante to have a variety in the means she possesses of divining by the cards.

Think for a moment of the endless variety there is in human nature. Surely this fact demands different methods of translating the hidden knowledge that lies in the depths of all. The bridge over which that knowledge must come is similar in all, but the methods of drawing it over the bridge are many. If one way of reading the cards for a consultant prove unsatisfactory, then be ready to try another. The means must be adjusted to the individual. Certainly the best plan will be to learn all the different ways of divination that I have given, and use them just as they appear most suitable to your consultant.

Here is an excellent way of laying out the cards which is easy to remember, simple to learn, and most satisfactory in its results. For a short reading when time is limited I can strongly recommend it. Its name is

YOUR LIFE

First remove the significator from the pack, and then let the consultant shuffle them a little. As the cards are drawn and not dealt, much shuffling is unnecessary. The cartomante then takes them and holds them loosely in the hand, face downwards,

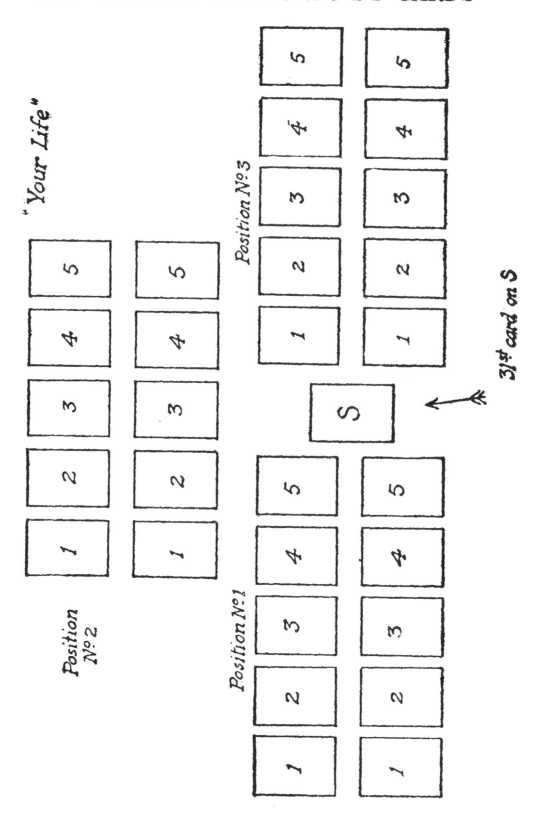

to the consultant who draws five cards haphazard from the pack, placing them as they are drawn, 1, 2, 3, 4, 5, face downwards in a row on the left of the significator. Five more cards are then drawn and placed in the same way, above it, (see diagram).

Draw five more cards and place at the head of the significator, also another row of five beneath it. In each case the first card of the drawing is put on the left. The third group is placed opposite the first on the right of the significator, the drawing of the cards being done in exactly the same way. There will be one card left over. This is placed upon the significator face upwards (as in diagram). It is a card showing something of importance to the consultant. If it is a court card, it indicates someone of great influence in the life, but much depends upon the appearance of the cards in the three positions, as to the interpretation to be given in the event of the card left over being a court card. I have seen this thirty-first card, the king of clubs. It has been an unmistakable confirmation of the group of cards representing " Life as it could be." It may be less decisive when it is not a court card, but it is never unimportant.

The positions of the cards are representative of: —

No. 1 position. " Your life as it is."
No. 2 position. " Your life as it might be."
No. 3 position. " Your life as it will be."

The drawing of the thirty cards being finished, the cartomante proceeds to turn up the packs of five beginning with those on the left of the significator (position No. 1). The ten cards in each position are now face upwards. Be careful that the order in which they are drawn is not disturbed.

The top row of position No. 1 is read in two sets of three, 1, 2, 3 — 3, 4, 5, the third card being used twice over. The row below is read in a similar way. Next proceed to deal with the cards above (position No. 2), and the cards to the right of the significator in like manner.

In each position the counting begins with the top card on the left hand.

YOUR LIFE

The reading and interpretation of the cards is in accordance with the respective positions they occupy. The general aspect of these groups of cards of ten should be carefully noted and taken into account in the reading; this in addition to the separate meaning given in the countings in the packs of three.

The thirty-first card is left for consideration until the end of the reading. It would undoubtedly be a bad omen if the nine of spades came out as the thirty-first card, even if the indications of the rest of the cards, in their respective positions, had been otherwise good. It would add to the gloom of the outlook if the cards in position No. 3, "Life as it will be," were chiefly spade cards. Things that tend to spoil the life and causes of unhappiness must be looked for in the general aspect of the cards in all three positions.

The cards, having been carefully studied and interpreted, are then taken up in pairs. Begin reading with the first card in the top row of No. 1 position and the first card of the row below. Read each pair separately.

Continue with No. 2 card and the card beneath it. Next No. 3, with No. 3 in the row below and so on.

Proceed next to pair the cards of Position No. 2 and Position No. 3 until the pairing is completed by the card of the significator and the thirty-first card.

My experience has proved the above method to be most reliable and well suited to the great majority of consultants.

THE FOUR KNAVES

Here is a method in which the four knaves are used as significators. They are representative of the twelve months of the year.

Remove the four knaves from the pack and place them as shown on the diagram.

Position 1. Knave of diamonds.
Position 2. Knave of hearts.
Position 3. Knave of clubs.
Position 4. Knave of spades.

The knave of diamonds stands for January, February, March.

The knave of hearts stands for April, May and June.

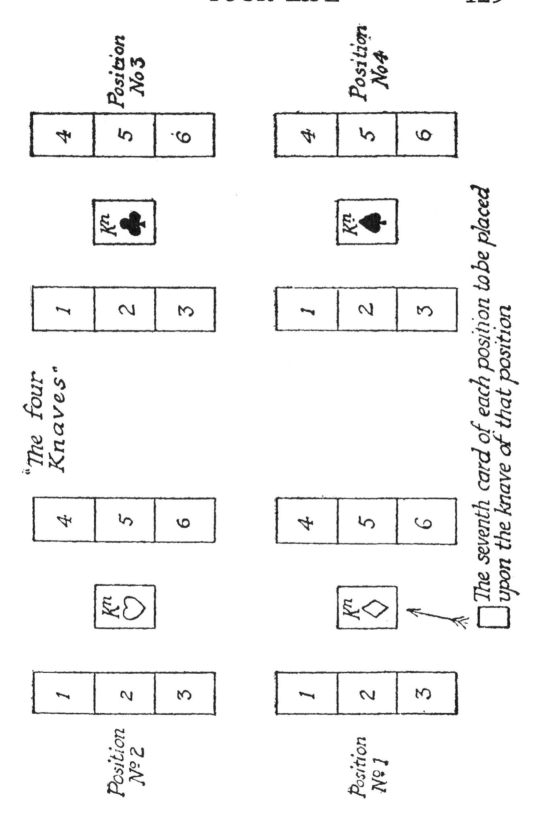

The knave of clubs stands for July, August and September.

The knave of spades stands for October, November and December.

There is no cut. The cards having been thoroughly shuffled are dealt as follows: —

The first card is placed face upwards on the left of and above the diamond knave. The second card beneath the first, and the third card beneath the second. The fourth card is put on the right of the knave of diamonds opposite the first card. The fifth goes below it, and the sixth place under the fifth. The seventh card is placed upon the knave (see diagram), as a card of final decision. Seven is a lucky number, and there are seven days in the week. This card can be used for the seventh day, as will be shown later.

The knave of hearts is the next position for the dealing of the seven cards, to be followed by the third position, the knave of clubs, the fourth, the knave of spades; each dealing of seven being done in exactly the same way, as in Position No. 1.

The counting in two pairs of three is done

first. The top left hand card, No. 1 card in the dealing, is used as No. 1 card in the count, with No. 2 card to form a link betwixt that and No. 3 card.

The top card on the right, No. 4 card, is the first card for the count on that side. This makes a reading in two threes.

No. 1 card on the left of the knave is again used as the first, and the counting now proceeds right round from No. 1 card to the seventh card, following the same order in which the pack was laid out, the top right hand card again being the fourth card.

The final counting of the seven cards is important, as it gives a summing up and decision on the general aspect in the several positions of the cards.

For instance, if the nine of spades were to come as the seventh card with the nine of diamonds in either of the groups of three around it, the outlook would be ominous, in fact a sign of death. If a court card appeared also, it would show — with a king — the death to be for a man, with a queen, the death for a woman. The probable time of the year in which the death takes place will be judged by the position in which these cards appear.

As I said previously, the seventh card may be further used as the seventh day of the week. Counting from:

    No. 1 card. Sunday.
    No. 2 card. Monday.
    No. 3 card. Tuesday.
    No. 4 card. Wednesday.
    No. 5 card. Thursday.
    No. 6 card. Friday.
    No. 7 card. Saturday.

This useful reading for the days of the week may be adjusted when the general aspect of the cards and the countings in threes and sevens has been done.

The method is as follows:—

Begin with the top left hand card of Position No. 1 (knave of diamonds) and the top left hand card of Position No. 2 (knave of hearts). Here we have two cards representing Sunday. No. 2 cards in the knave of diamonds and knave of hearts group gives us Monday. No. 3 cards in No. 1 and No. 2 positions gives us Tuesday. No. 4 cards in the two positions stand for

Wednesday. No. 5 cards for Thursday and No. 6 cards for Friday. No. 7 cards in both positions gives us Saturday.

The cards are read for the seven days of the week in exactly the same way in group No. 3 (knave of clubs) and group 4 (knave of spades). The top left hand card in each case represents Sunday.

Many of us have days we consider lucky or unlucky, as the case may be. In this method given above, one can find out how the cards verify our luck, or lack of luck, upon those particular days.

For example, supposing the nine of hearts to be the No. 1 card in the knave of diamonds group, with the king of hearts as the No. 1 card in the knave of hearts group, Sunday would be shown in this case as a day of pleasure and realised wishes with regard to this man (king of hearts) with whom there is much happiness and affection.

Or again let us suppose the ace of clubs to be the fourth card in the knave of clubs group, with the queen of hearts as the fourth card in the group below (knave of spades). It will be seen that Wednesday would be the day for some pleasant news to come in a letter from the queen of hearts.

Once more, supposing the queen of spades to be the sixth card in position No. 3, with the eight of spades as the sixth card in position No. 4. It will be seen that Friday is a day of trouble for a spade woman. Probably a slight illness. The card above would in each case be a guide as to the extent of the trouble. With bad cards in these positions, the predicted trouble would be increased. Good cards in these positions would show that the trouble was not serious and only temporary.

A consultant may find it interesting to have special attention given to the groups in which her birthday falls. Special notice must be directed to where the court cards come in the position in which the birth month occurs. If with good cards, such as hearts, clubs or diamonds (without spades) then this would show good and influential friends or relatives.

If with money cards, good presents, or money, would be shown.

It is a good sign if the card representing

the consultant appears in the group of cards in which the birth month comes. If the wish card, or kings, or ten of hearts, came in this group, it would give promise of much happiness, and being "born under a lucky star."

Taking up the cards in pairs gives an extended reading, which will probably be found to endorse, as it were, the previous interpretations.

Sometimes the pairs may foretell a small, or trivial event, likely to occur shortly. The pairs are made as follows: —

Beginning with No. 1 group take up

No. 1 card with No. 4 card.
No. 2 card with No. 5 card.
No. 3 card with No. 6 card.

Leave the seventh card in each position until the end.

Positions No. 3 and No. 4 are dealt with in a similar way, each pair forming a reading. Next take up the seventh card in No. 1 Position and the seventh card in No. 2 Position. The pair are read together. Act similarly with the seventh cards in No. 3 and No. 4 Positions.

I have found this method of reading greatly affected by my consultant, as if correctly carried out it is invariably accurate and always interesting.

Here is another short and simple method of laying out the cards.

The consultant shuffles and cuts the cards as usual.

The cartomante then takes them up in the order in which they are cut and interprets.

The cards are dealt face downwards in two rows of four on the left. Next two more rows of four under the first row, but not touching it. Continue a similar dealing of the cards on the right. Place them opposite, but not touching, the eight on the left. The cards in each pack should be noticed as a whole, with regard to their several positions. A glance will show much of the meaning of the cards in their positions, quite apart from the counting.

Count in three pairs, 1 and 2, 2 and 3, 3 and 4, in each row of four cards.

Begin with Position No. 1. The positions represent the following conditions: —

No. 1. Things of to-day.
No. 2. Things of to-morrow.
No. 3. Things of joy.
No. 4. Things of sorrow.

Though not really necessary, the consultant may shuffle the cards between each dealing of the separate packs. This is a mere matter of personal choice.

Positions No. 1 and No. 2, representing things of to-day and things of to-morrow, must not be considered as being strictly limited to those two days. The events indicated might not develop so rapidly, though the chances are that they will.

The cards having been read, they are taken up in pairs. The first card of the top row in Position No. 1 with the first card of Position No. 2. Pair the second card in Position No. 1 with the second card in Position No. 2, continuing thus until all the cards in the four positions have been paired.

138 TELLING FORTUNES BY CARDS

When only a brief time can be spared by a consultant, here is a short and useful method.

The consultant shuffles the cards, then hands them to the cartomante. She holds them loosely, face downwards, whilst the consultant withdraws seven cards from the pack and places them, face downwards, in a row upon the table. Seven more cards are then drawn and placed below the first line of seven. Next five cards are drawn and laid below the second row.

Before drawing the cards from the pack the consultant should be told what each drawing represents.

    1. The wish.
    2. The attainment.
    3. The consolation.

When the drawing of the cards is finished the cartomante turns them up in the order in which they were drawn, and reads them in relation to their positions.

For instance, if the wish card comes out in the first line of seven cards as the third, with the nine of spades as the seventh card, and with a court card as the sixth card, it will at once be seen that there is no hope of the wish being fulfilled.

The court card, as the sixth, would indicate through whom the failure of the wish being realised would be brought about.

If lucky cards came in the pack of five, representing the consolation, it would be encouraging and hopeful, apart from the thing wished for.

The three lines of cards are counted as follows: — The two lines of seven 1, 2, 3, and 4, 5, 6, 7. Making the third and seventh form a link.

The line of five cards is counted 1, 2, 3, 3, 4, 5, using the third card twice.

CHAPTER X

THE SHORT ENQUIRY

A Simple Method for Beginners. Significator on Table. Drawing of the Cards by Consultant. Another Method Called "Past, Present and Future" (see diagram). "The Aces." How to Place Them. A Good Omen, the Wish Card and the Significator Coming Out in the Same Pack. "The Fifteen." Dealing in Three. A "Wish Way." A Method for the Twenty-four hours. Trivial Events and Important Happenings Side by Side. "The Day's Events." What to Note. Whole Pack Held in Hands. Indications to be Expected. The Simplicity and Reliability of This Method for the Happenings of the Daily Life. Another Method for the Twenty-four Hours. How to Draw the Cards. Reading in Pairs. An easy Means of Arriving at an Accurate Prognostication. A Useful Method for Those Who are Forgetful. A Favourite Means of Divination. An Example Case.

THERE is a short and very simple way of using the cards called "The Short Enquiry," which we will now consider, as some may like to use it occasionally. It is sometimes useful and inter-

THE SHORT ENQUIRY 141

esting, after the general fortune has been predicted by the fuller methods of doing the cards.

Place the significator on the table, then let the consultant draw seven cards at random from the pack, the cartomante holding the pack loosely in the hand with

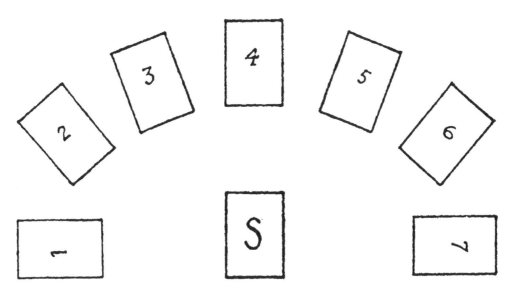

"The Short enquiry"

the cards face downwards. Each card as it is drawn must be placed face downwards on the table, round the significator, as shown in the diagram and in the order in which it is drawn. The consultant again draws seven more cards, in the same way, covering each card in the same order — beginning at No. 1 card on the left. The cartomante then reads the pairs, in the order in which they are placed, for example: —

1. Nine of diamonds   Eight of clubs (reversed); a telegram.
2. Ace of diamonds   Ten of diamonds; a railway journey.
3. Knave of hearts   Ten of spades; separation from a friend or lover.
4. Seven of spades   Eight of diamonds; a change of weather.
5. Seven of hearts   Eight of spades; domestic troubles.
6. Ace of clubs   Seven of diamonds; a parcel.
7. Nine of clubs   Nine of spades; a great disappointment.

This way of telling the cards will be found much easier for beginners than those methods which have a larger number of cards to form the reading. The interpretation of the pairs is naturally easier than those in fours, though practice soon reduces the difficulty. In time a glance at the cards reveals the whole

THE SHORT ENQUIRY 143

meaning. Nevertheless, the method just given of reading the cards in pairs is a satisfactory method when time is limited, whether for beginners or otherwise.

Another method of reading the cards with the significator placed in the centre may be given. It is a more comprehensive reading than the preceding one, as all the cards are used. This method is called

"PAST, PRESENT, FUTURE."

The card representing the consultant is placed on the table. The remaining thirty-one cards must be thoroughly shuffled and cut in three packs. The cut is read and interpreted to the consultant. Then two cards are placed face downwards on the significator card. Next place a card at the head, a card at the foot, a card at the right, and one on the left. Put a card aside above the head, but not touching the cards at the head. Continue this way of dealing until all the cards are finished. There will be five cards at the head, ten on the significator, and four in each of the other sets of cards.

144 TELLING FORTUNES BY CARDS

The five cards over the representative card of the consultant indicate what may be expected to happen very speedily. Those on the right show events and conditions

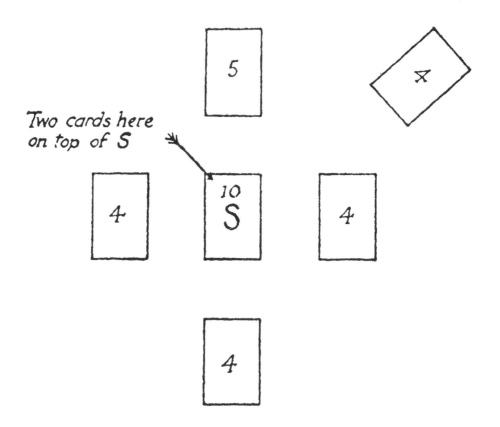

"Past, Present, Future"

not far distant. Those on the left tell of things in the past. The cards at the feet indicate plans and their hindrances. A diagram given shows the method of dealing the

THE SHORT ENQUIRY 145

cards, which is sometimes found a little troublesome at first, but it is soon mastered. It is very fortunate if the wish card comes in any of the packs without spade cards being included. This shows attainment of wishes and plans successfully carried out. If the nine of spades comes with the nine of hearts it is a bad outlook. It means a failure of that which would lead to your desires. There is a good prospect if the five cards above the significator have the wish card and other heart cards; or diamonds and heart cards above it, without any spade cards to diminish the good.

Having laid out the cards in the order given, next read the several packs with regard to their positions, the near future, the more distant future, the past, the present. Then take the cards on the top of the significator and divide them into two packs of five, dealing the two packs from left to right. Those on the left show what events are likely to affect the future — things occurring to help or delay. The pack of five cards on the right show the influence of those who will be in the life of the consultant, the good arising from them, etc. Next take the four cards which have been put aside at the head of the significator. These are the cards of judgment and final decisions, indicating that which must be. If these four cards were all good cards, after a display of mixed cards without any very decidedly hopeful outlook, then these four good cards would throw the balance on to the side of a hopeful interpretation of the whole reading. It is important to remember that four cards together are read in three pairs — 1 and 2, 2 and 3, 3 and 4. Five cards to be read in two threes — 1, 2, 3, and 3, 4, 5.

Another method in which the four aces are used to foreshow the success or otherwise of projects or plans, may be given: —

"THE ACES."

Remove the four aces from the pack. Place the ace of clubs at the head, the ace of spades at the foot, the ace of hearts on the right, the ace of diamonds on the left. The remaining twenty-eight cards are now shuffled thoroughly, and during this process the consultant must concentrate the mind

THE SHORT ENQUIRY

on what is most wished for. There is no cut. The consultant hands the pack back to the cartomante, and the cards are then dealt round as follows: — The first card on the ace of clubs; the second on the ace of spades; the third on the ace of hearts; the fourth on the ace of diamonds. Continue dealing the cards in this order until they are used up, having put seven cards on each of the four aces. Turn up each pack and read the cards. It will be a good omen, and an indication of gaining your wish, if the wish card and significator come out in the same pack. If these two cards are found to be separated, then first read the pack in which the significator is found, and interpret it with regard to its position. Next read the pack which has the wish card in it, also with regard to its position.

1. Ace of clubs — Success, achievement.
2. Ace of spades — Failure, obstacles.
3. Ace of hearts — the home, social pleasures, friends.
4. Ace of diamonds — Business transaction.

This must be done in each case. It will

be a sure sign of the wish being realised if the wish card comes out in the pack on the ace of clubs, as this is a card symbolising victory. If the wish card is on the diamond ace, it will mean triumph through money. If on the heart ace, the wish probably comes through the help of others. If on the spade ace, there is little to be hoped for. What you already possess is likely to be all you will have, at any rate for a long time. If the nine of spades comes out with the card of the significator, or wish card, everything is spoiled; wishes thwarted, projects failing, hopes disappointed. This is a simple but reliable method of prognostication for a consultant who wishes for information on the subject of gaining a desire, or succeeding in an undertaking,

Here is a shorter way of placing the cards, as only fifteen are used. It is a good method of obtaining knowledge as to the fulfilment of a wish.

"THE FIFTEEN."

First put the significator on the table, then let the consultant shuffle the cards well, wishing all the time. Taking three cards

THE SHORT ENQUIRY 149

from the top of the pack, place them at the head of the significator. Then place three cards at the feet; three on the right, three on the left, and three on the significator. The three cards at the head of the significator are for good fortune in the present; those at the feet, for luck that you may have had and still enjoy; those at the right show that which you may hope for of good luck in the future; the cards on the left show hindrances and what is obstructing your path. The three cards on the significator show that which is, or will shortly be, crossing his path.

The cards must be taken up in their several packs of threes, and interpreted in regard to the positions they occupy. If the ace of clubs not reversed, or ten of hearts, or wish card, comes out at the head of the significator, it is a very hopeful sign, and promises well for the fulfilment of the wish. The wish would also be obtained if these cards came out in the packs on the right, or on the top of the significator; but if the nine of spades were to appear in the same pack, it would counterbalance the good cards, and deny the wish being gratified.

There is a simple, but excellent method of reading the cards for things likely to occur within the day. I have found it a very reliable way of prediction. Of course it happens sometimes that events and conditions to be seen in the cards do not come immediately, but certainly they are very near, and much of what is told is actually coming about on that day. It may be, for instance, that a letter with good or bad news, as the case may be, is seen in the cards, but does not reach the consultant that day.

It is found that the letter was in process of being written at the time, or on the day on which the consultant is inquiring of the cards by this method. Trivial events will naturally come out in this way of doing the cards, also big events will appear side by side with these minor happenings.

The meanings of the cards must be strictly adhered to in the interpretations, quite irrespective of what may seem to be a much more likely course of events in the life of the consultant. The knowledge revealing these happenings is to be trusted, and must be translated as it appears. For those who

THE SHORT ENQUIRY 151

have a belief in this knowledge being transmitted to the cards and thus symbolised by them, this method of the day's events will be found most useful and full of interest. There are some who make a regular practice of ascertaining the probable events of the day by this method. It is certainly a good way of remembering that " forewarned is forearmed."

" THE DAY'S EVENTS."

First remove the significator, then hand the cards to the consultant to shuffle. When this has been thoroughly done, let the consultant replace the card representing herself anywhere in the pack that she may choose. Then the whole pack, with the significator's card now replaced, is taken by the cartomante and read. First find the significator's card, and see in what position it appears to be. Note if the significator faces good or bad cards, or if she turns her back on them, if spade cards, or spades and diamonds, are ahead, or if the back of the significator is turned towards them, thus indicating troubles and dangers passed by. Watch the cards in combination for such signs as an invitation, a doctor, domestic troubles, breakages, or loss of valuables, meetings with friends, letters, weather, plans, etc. The whole pack is held in the hands, and the cards just moved along as necessary.

Another method of doing the cards for the twenty-four hours may be given. In this way the full pack of thirty-two cards is used. The cartomante holds them loosely in the hand, face downwards, towards the consultant, who then draws out nine cards. She places the first on the left hand of the cartomante, face downwards on the table; the second card next to the first, but not touching it, and so on round the table, till the nine cards are drawn. She then draws out nine more cards, beginning with the tenth card which she places on the first card. She continues in this order until the eighteenth card is reached. The cards are then taken up in pairs and read, beginning with the pack on the left of the semi-circle, interpreting the pairs with regard to the positions they occupy — as follows: —

THE SHORT ENQUIRY

1. Someone I shall meet.
2. Someone I care for.
3. Someone who annoys me.
4. Something that consoles me.
5. Something awaiting me.
6. Something that helps me.
7. Something surprising.
8. Something I wish for.
9. Something nice happening.

The first pair on the left will therefore refer to someone whom the consultant may expect to meet during the day. For example, the king of spades and eight of hearts, a widower. The second pair in rotation refers to someone dear to the consultant. The king of hearts and eight of diamonds, a fair man much in the thoughts of the consultant, with whom there will be a speedy meeting. The third pair has reference to that which annoys, queen of clubs and eight of spades indicate something troublesome with a medium coloured woman. The fourth pair speaks of consolation. Ace of clubs and ten of clubs bring most fortunate and pleasant news. The fifth pair refers to that which awaits the consultant. Seven of diamonds and queen of hearts shows a present from a fair woman. The sixth pair refers to something helpful. King of diamonds and eight of clubs, here is a fair man; a delightful and valuable friend. The seventh pair has reference to a surprise. Ace of diamonds and ten of diamonds, a railway journey is coming. The eighth pair shows a wish. Nine of hearts and nine of diamonds, the wish will be fulfilled without delay. The ninth pair refers to a pleasant occurrence. Seven of clubs and seven of spades, plans with regard to a change are being arranged.

This way of consulting the cards will usually be found popular, as will the other methods given for defining the events of the day. It is easy for those who consult the cards to remember events predicted to occur within a very short time. When such events as have been foretold occur, as they most certainly will, whilst the predictions are still in the mind of the consultant, it is likely to induce a feeling of respect for the cards and their revealings.

There are many who are interested in the

reading of their cards, but except for those events which come almost immediately, they remember little or nothing of what they have been told, therefore, when the predicted occurrences befall them there is no recollection of the provision and prophecy of the cards! The method of reading the cards just given, or "The Day's Events," will be found most convincing to those who are constitutionally forgetful.

CHAPTER XI

THE SMALLER CARDS

The Full Pack of Fifty-two Cards. The Significance of the Lesser Cards. Some Mixed Combinations. The Necessity of Committing These Meanings to Memory. A Method of Laying Out the Cards. The Reading. The Count. The Significance of the First, Second, Third, and Fourth Row in Relation to the Consultant. The Take Up and Pairing Not of Primary Importance. Opinions as to the Frequency of Consulting the Cards. The Necessity for Different Packs. Another System for the Fifty-two Cards. The Advisability of a Beginner not attempting to Learn This and Previous Method. Meanings of the Cards. Some Mixed Combinations and Their Meanings. The Cards to be Displayed and Counted in the Same Manner as Given in the First Method of Using the Fifty-two Cards. Another Method of Using the Full Pack Called "The Eight-Fold Sixes." The Significator in the Centre. The Dealing as Shown in the Diagram. The Four Positions Representing "Hope," "Doubt," "Fears," "Achievements." The Importance of Reading Each Position Pack in its Right Order. The Pairing. Another Way of Using the Fifty-two Cards. The Six Packs and Their Significance. The Reading in Pairs to be Interpreted in Relation to the Order in which They are Placed.

THERE may be readers who would like to use the full pack of fifty-two cards; for those the meanings of these cards are given.

THE SMALLER CARDS

DIAMONDS.

	RIGHT.	REVERSED.
Six.	Optimism.	Domestic annoyance.
Five.	Good fortune.	Legal Proceedings.
Four.	Social Pleasures.	Pleasant happenings.
Three.	Business.	Separation.
Two.	Money.	Amazement.

HEARTS.

Six.	The Past.	The future.
Five.	Marriage prospects.	An arrival.
Four.	A message.	Grumbling.
Three.	Attainment.	Papers.
Two.	Affection.	Obstacles.

CLUBS.

Six.	A present.	Much effort.
Five.	One dear to you.	Dissipation.
Four.	Pleasant happenings.	Delay.
Three.	Careful management.	Desired position.
Two.	Children.	News and letters.

SPADES.

Six.	A long journey or across water.	Surprise.
Five.	Bereavement.	Sadness.
Four.	Loneliness.	Suggestions.
Three.	Disagreement.	Chaos.
Two.	Friendship.	Someone averse to you.

SOME COMBINATIONS.

Four sixes.	Sound advice.	Difference of opinion.
Four fives.	Be cautious.	Disloyalty.
Four fours.	Reserve.	Ability.
Four threes.	Strategy.	Loss of hope.
Four twos.	A piece of news.	Indifference.

	RIGHT.	REVERSED.
Three sixes.	A generous person.	Doubting.
Three fives.	Position.	Money.
Three fours.	Calamity.	A suspicious person.

THE SMALLER CARDS

Three threes.	Successful doings.	A doubtful character.
Three twos.	An enemy.	Fear.
Two sixes.	Gaining.	Pleasure.
Two fives.	Worry.	Haste.
Two fours.	Recklessness.	Extravagance.
Two threes.	Achievement.	Losses, obstructions.
Two twos.	A small gratification.	Reliable character.

It is of course necessary to have a method of counting for the whole pack, other than that which has already been given. Having learned the meanings of the lesser cards, we may now consider the method of laying out the fifty-two cards for the use of those who wish to employ the full pack.

The cards are shuffled and cut (the significator being left in the pack). Read the cut, interpreting the three packs — (the cutting is done as in other ways of consultation by the cards — 1, 2, 3,) with regard to something near at hand of some importance for the consultant. Take up the cards again in the order in which they were cut, holding them face downwards in the left hand and dealing with the right. The first card is to be put on the left of the table, the second card next to it, and so on dealing to the right until there are thirteen cards in a row, with the faces upwards. Then begin again on the left, dealing a second row of thirteen cards. Continue doing this until there are four rows of cards with thirteen cards in each row.

THE READING OF THE CARDS.

Counting the first card as one, pass on to the fifth card, then to the ninth, from the ninth to the thirteenth, which will bring you to the end of the first row. The cards one and five, five and nine, nine and thirteen, should be read together. Next read the meanings to be found in the second row of cards, counting in the same way. Then begin with the third row in the same manner. Lastly the fourth row, giving separate readings from each row.

The first row has special relation to the consultant, his ideas, plans, etc.

THE SMALLER CARDS 161

The second row gives indication of his finances, business, possessions.

The third row refers to relatives, friends, acquaintances, associates, correspondents.

The fourth and last row shows the result of projects, the final issue of things, ultimate results.

Any doubt as to an event or circumstance arising from the reading, may be solved by counting from the significator to the fifth, ninth, and thirteenth cards, the reading being done from left to right. If a question arises as to general prospects, or money affairs, the counting and reading must then be made from the nine of hearts. Counting in this way from the house card would give a decision as to removals, change, domestic and family affairs.

Having been thus counted and read in this way, the cards are taken up and read in pairs in the following manner. The first card of the top row and the last card of the fourth row are taken up, one with the left hand, the other with the right, placed together and read, the two cards forming a reading. The second card in the top row, and the twelfth card in the fourth row are then taken up together and read. Continue this till all the cards have thus been coupled and interpreted.

Frequently it is found that the coupling of the cards after a general reading endorses, as it were, the main reading. Sometimes the pairs mean events that will not affect the consultant in any way beyond the fact that the hearing of them makes a certain impression on the mind. It often happens that in the case of court cards, it is indicative of visitors to the house. This applies to the pairing of the cards in the first method given, when the thirty-two cards only are used.

These pairings should not be regarded as of primary importance. It is only practice and experience that can give the cartomante a sense of proportion, and value to the events and conditions which occur in the cards.

This is sometimes a matter of difficulty, but the remedy is practice.

It is said by some authorities that no one should consult the cards more often than once

THE SMALLER CARDS 163

in every three months. There are few people however, who will thus limit their inquiries from the cards. It is far more usual for those who find interest and pleasure in this form of what is popularly described as " fortune telling," to seek information through their mediumship each time an opportunity arises. It is so tempting just to see if there is anything nice going to happen since the last time the cards were read!

It is, I think, most necessary to warn those who like their cards read very often, that the trivial doings and events of daily life will most certainly be in evidence, otherwise I do not see any need for restricting the inquirer's natural desire for information, which is unobtainable except through some means of bringing the hidden knowledge to the surface — such as the cards. But let all decide for themselves. Personally, I use my cards regularly, and find them most accurate. The days would be something of a blank without any intercourse with my friends — the cards; for curiously, it is as friends that one regards them, even when they seem to be gathering into their revelations all the inconvenient and unwished for statements — with the most undesired events. It may leave you dismayed for a time, but you must, in spite of it, have a feeling of profound respect and admiration for the candor which has the courage to be truthfully unpleasant!

There is a very personal element of interest in predictions of circumstances and events to come. There is also the greater interest in the powers of the subconsciousness with all its store of knowledge, being capable of interpretation by means of the simple handling of the cards and the translation of their meanings. Surely it is a supremely interesting and wonderful fact.

There is one rather important point to be mentioned for those who use the cards very often for themselves and others — do not always use the same pack. It is advisable to keep one pack for your own use, for if the cartomante has constantly used the pack which is to be used for those who are inquirers of the cards, it will certainly be found that meanings are identified by the cartomante as belonging to personal events, and nothing to do with the consultant. Cards used incessantly by one person seem to become so impregnated with that personality, it becomes nearly impossible to be quite free from a mixed element when others handle the cards.

For a cartomante who uses the cards regularly, I recommend that a pack be kept entirely for personal use. This is a precaution well worth taking.

I will now give a method shown to me by an Irish friend, who has found it most reliable. It is useful to those who prefer to use the whole pack to have a choice in the manner of their employment.

As the meanings attached to the various cards in this system are different from those given in the previous chapter, it would be advisable not to attempt both, but to choose one. Trying both would only lead to confusion in the case of a beginner. Only an old hand can grasp both systems and keep each apart. The meanings of the cards must first be committed to memory before reading them is attempted. The meanings are as follows:—

CLUBS.

	RIGHT.	REVERSED.
Ace.	Good news.	Papers, documents.
Ten.	A journey.	An outing.
Nine.	Business.	Delays.
Eight.	Short journey.	A walk.
Seven.	Success.	Uncertainty.
Six.	Vexation.	Disturbance.
Five.	Talk, discussion.	Disagreement.
Four.	A strange bed.	Bad dreams, wakefulness.
Three.	Letters, news.	Delayed or unwelcome news.
Two.	Shaking hands.	An introduction.

DIAMONDS.

	RIGHT.	REVERSED.
Ace.	A good present.	A small gift.
Ten.	Money.	Pleasant outlook—with spades, pain.
Nine.	Money, business.	Speed, decision.
Eight.	Jewellery.	Clothes, furniture.
Seven.	Animals.	A bicycle.
Six.	Pleasure.	Boredom.
Five.	Money settlement.	Annoyance ahead.
Four.	A friend.	Money.

THE SMALLER CARDS 167

Three.	A pleasant meeting.	Quarrel with a friend.
Two.	A surprise.	Gossip.

HEARTS.

	RIGHT.	REVERSED.
Ace.	The home.	Great affection.
Ten.	Happiness.	Lucky changes with ace, marriage.
Nine.	The wish.	Someone dear to you.
Eight.	Affection.	Friendship.
Seven.	Lesser wish.	Jealousy.
Six.	Pleasure.	Social duties.
Five.	Present.	Domestics.
Four.	Invitation.	A refusal.
Three.	Time, weeks or days.	Arrivals.
Two.	Time, days.	Departures.

SPADES.

	RIGHT.	REVERSED.
Ace.	Sorrow.	Ace, with 9, 7, 4, 2, of spades, death.
Ten.	Sea.	Illness.
Nine.	Disappointment.	Loss.
Eight.	A distance away.	Night.

Seven.	Removal.	Indecision.
Six.	Child or relation.	Difficulties.
Five.	With 2 and 3 spades, sharp words.	Domestic difficulties.
Four.	A sick bed.	Trials.
Three.	With 3 of clubs, tears.	Minor worries.
Two.	Motor or carriage.	A parcel.

SOME MIXED COMBINATIONS AND THEIR MEANINGS.

Nine of clubs (reversed), seven of spades (reversed) — disappointment.

Ace of clubs, five of clubs — Talk leading to profitable conclusions.

Six of clubs, four of clubs — Vexation when on a visit.

Ten of clubs (reversed), diamonds (reversed) — A very pleasant outing.

Eight of clubs, five of diamonds — Short journey on financial business

Two of clubs, two of diamonds — Surprising and unexpected meeting.

Ace of diamonds, three of clubs — A good present by post.

THE SMALLER CARDS 169

Ten of diamonds, three of hearts — Good money prospects near at hand.

Nine of diamonds (reversed), four of spades — Sudden illness.

Eight of diamonds, five of hearts — A present of jewellery.

Four of diamonds, three of hearts—Arrival of a friend.

Ace of hearts, ace of spades — Sadness in the home.

Ten of spades, four of spades — Seasickness.

Seven of spades, seven of hearts — Increasing affection.

The cards may be laid out and counted in exactly the same way as I have described in Chapter X as a method of using the whole pack. The kings, queens and knaves of each suit represent the persons and their thoughts, as in other ways of card reading.

I will now describe another way of displaying fifty-two cards. It is called

THE EIGHT-FOLD SIXES.

First remove the significator from the pack and place this card in the centre. The

"The eight-fold Sixes"

3 cards left out

THE SMALLER CARDS 171

consultant then thoroughly shuffles the cards, and also turns them from end to end, as the meanings are different when reversed.

The pack is then cut into three and the cartomante will pick up the cards in the order in which they were cut and read and interpret the cut, finally laying out the cards in eight rows of six each.

The first card is placed above and to the left of the significator. The second card goes next to it, and then a third card. Continue dealing in this way until six cards are in a row. Next lay six more cards below (see diagram), placing the first card of the second row under the first card in the row above. In exactly the same order put two rows of six cards below the significator.

To the left, and at right angles to the significator, place two rows of six, the first card being placed in the top row (as shown in diagram). Repeat in exactly the same order on the right of the significator. The first card being in this case placed above the significator, the dealing proceeds downwards, as the numbered cards show in the diagram. Three cards are left over from the dealing, and they are placed face downwards on the table until the reading of the other cards is finished. The three are then taken up and read as a final verdict.

If the prognostication has been only fairly good, a favourable decision can be given if these three cards are hopeful.

THE FOUR POSITIONS.

The four positions represent four conditions:—

    No. 1. Your hope for the future.
    No. 2. Your doubts in the present.
    No. 3. Your fears in the past.
    No. 4. Your achievements to come.

The row of twelve cards should be carefully studied as to their appearance as a whole, and in regard to their respective positions before beginning to count.

Each position must be taken in its right order, and the counting is done in two sets of threes, in each separate row in the four positions, 1, 2 and 3, 4, 5 and 6.

Having exhausted the cards in this manner, take them up in pairs, beginning with No. 1

THE SMALLER CARDS 173

card of the first row, and No. 1 card of the second row in position No. 1. Bring them together and form a reading. Continue in this way until each card is paired. Pair the cards in No. 2, No. 3 and No. 4 positions in a similar manner. Finally take up the three cards left over from the dealing and interpret them as a final decision.

Here is another way of using the pack of fifty-two.

The consultant thoroughly shuffles the cards and cuts them into three packs.

The cartomante takes them up in the order in which they were cut, and deals them into six separate packs of eight cards. There will be four cards left over. These may be interpreted as things of little importance to the consultant. Perhaps nothing more than a trifling incident that has brought a little vexation.

The dealing of the cards begins on the left of the dealer. They are placed face upwards in two rows of four cards. Below place two more rows of four cards, and a similar two rows beneath that again. It is important that these packs should not touch each other, otherwise confusion in the reading will result, but the two rows forming each separate pack may be touching.

On the right, opposite the first pack of eight, place three more packs of eight cards; dealing them in exactly the same way as before. The six packs represent:—

No. 1. The lady herself.
No. 2. Her home.
No. 3. Her health.
No. 4. Her wish.
No. 5. Her friends.
No. 6. Her wealth.

The cards are read in pairs, the top card with the one below it; beginning with position No. 1. Read the pairs thus in each separate position in the order in which they are placed. Each pair forms a reading and their meanings must be interpreted in relation to the position they occupy.

CHAPTER XII

THE OUIJA BOARD

The Discovery of the Subconscious Self. Divination by a Glass Tumbler. How to Employ the Tumbler. How to Acquire the Letters Needed in this Method and How to Lay Them Out.

As regards psychic matters, we are all at school, an infant school or kindergarten. We are compelled to use symbols in order to learn the simplest details, our A.B.C. of mystic lore. Yet even those childish toys, such as " Ouija " boards, which are made by the million in America, and at the present moment are the most popular children's and adults' toys in America yield certain satisfactory results. Were it not so America would not have found it necessary to erect

"Ouija" factories and start "Ouija" companies.

Perhaps the greatest discovery that has yet come to us from America is that of the subconscious self. It was not really a new discovery. From time immemorial it has been taught and understood in the East, but we as a nation had passed it by and failed to realise its over-whelming importance. America's gift to us was the resurrecting of this all-important teaching, and she gave it to us in the form of " New Thought " books.

Those works emphasized the fact that we possess certain powers which form no part of our active thinking mind, or what we might call our everyday intelligence.

Through some avenue that we have never understood, we get flashes of intuition, gleams of second sight, suggestions, and warnings of trouble to come, recollections of events that we had forgotten for years. Often when we are thinking of something quite different, an impression arises in our minds, and we wonder where it has come from.

This seems to indicate a source of knowledge within us that discloses its presence quite by accident as it were. We are beginning to realise what an enormous gain it would be to us if we could tap this source of knowledge at will. This source of knowledge we say lives in our subconsciousness. No man yet knows what this subconsciousness is, but all the scientists are trying to find out.

This brings me to the real use of divination by cards, the use of Planchette and all the other mediums we employ in our kindergarten. They are a means of tapping this source of knowledge. They form a medium through which, in some way we do not yet understand, particles of this hidden knowledge can be brought to the surface.

Undoubtedly this hidden knowledge is far more easily conveyed to the surface, and recognised and translated by some than by others. Curiously enough it is by no means always those people who would appear externally to be the most likely to possess this strong affinity with their subconsciousness who know anything of it at all. Again the most unlikely people see ghosts and testify to what they have witnessed. Even so it often comes about that those whom we would be inclined to judge as hardened materialists have acquired the power of drawing from the inexhaustible store of their subconsciousness, and needless to say they profit exceedingly by their unique advantage.

Amongst the various different mediums through which knowledge may be obtained, the medium of the tumbler is by no means to be despised.

Of course there are people whom the tumbler simply will not tolerate, and it is apt to impress its dislike in rather forcible language on these occasions. There are others for whom it will not move at all, merely remaining *in statu quo,* sulkily refusing to move towards its mode of expression, the alphabet.

The first time I ever saw the tumbler used as a means of divination was a few years before the war, and under the most inappropriate conditions, or so it seemed to me.

I was summoned to an interview with a

certain very great lady who was temporarily sojourning in the North of Scotland.

There were highland games taking place that afternoon, and I was bidden to arrive at an hotel to which she had driven an hour before the games were due to begin.

At the appointed moment I was ushered straight into a small inn parlour, and a strange sight met my eyes. The great personage sat at a round table from which the cloth had been removed, and before her were scattered the letters of the alphabet. Her fingers were laid upon an inverted tumbler. She took no notice of my arrival, not even glancing round, but one of the three ladies present advanced with finger on lip, and signed to me to be seated.

From my chair I watched the tumbler with remarkable agility dart from letter to letter. One of the ladies stood beside the table and kept careful note with paper and pencil, and I could see that she had quite a long script already written.

After about a quarter of an hour, during which no one had spoken, the activities of the tumbler abruptly ceased. The great personage lay back in her chair and held out her hand for the script. Its perusal occupied her for another rather long period. At last she heaved a sigh which sounded like relief. Turning to me she gave pleasant greeting.

She explained that she had just received important letters which had disturbed her and required elucidation, and that she could not rest until she had used the tumbler to discover the truth.

She informed me that the tumbler was the surest medium for divination, and that she had used it for years without meeting with a single failure.

It occurred to me then and there that if this remarkably intelligent woman could get real satisfaction by this means of divination others could do likewise. On inquiry I found that tumblers were used to a much greater extent than I had any idea of, and as they are becoming more popular every day I have included in this book directions as to how they should be used.

To begin with they are sometimes a source of anxiety. The tumbler has the same fiendish delight that a talking parrot has in placing you in an awkward position. Both are capable of plunging you into despair just when you are particularly anxious that nothing shall be said to alarm or shock the susceptibilities of those who happen to be around you. This is the congenial moment for the tumbler, or the parrot, both are ambitious to bring forth a large D—— quite unmistakably ending in ——n. It is most awkward.

I may mention that when I began touching the tumbler, in the most friendly way possible, it was the unfailing signal for this impossible word to be spelt out rapidly. Time has healed that sore point. I think I had better explain that there was always another touching the tumbler at the same time. So it was probably the mixture it could not face without first expostulating! It had an expression it kept on purpose for a " flapper " sister — who jeered openly at it — " You, Mary, are a bad egg." It took great pride apparently in having found a term so brief and yet so descriptive, for it was repeated several times, and it rocked violently on the table afterwards exactly as if it had been laughing with delight at its own ready wit!

But this of course is only one side of the tumbler and its habits. It can be very serious and striking in its prophecies. There is no doubt whatever that much depends on those who are handling it, strong magnetism or the utter lack of magnetism affecting it very much. I have seen it write rapidly, and with a vivid power of description, for two magnetic persons. It often singles out one person, whose name it spells to begin with, and all information is directed to that person, not always one of those who are touching it at the time. The tumbler is influenced by aura, I mean the atmosphere created by those in the room, and the apparent perverseness of the tumbler, or its absolute refusal to write anything but nonsense, is often caused by the atmosphere being disturbing or uncongenial to it. When this is so it will probably display much energy in jerky movements, going from letter to letter, quite irrespective of any attempt at words or sentences. Sometimes a gentle remonstrance, or a more forcible method of argument, stirs it up to a sense of duty, and it makes a supreme effort to give a display of its powers.

Occasionally the tumbler deals entirely with abstract matters; it discourses on general subjects which are interesting and often worthy of an appreciative audience. The tumbler exhibits variety in its talk, often it is an excellent conversationalist, sometimes it adopts a symbolic type of utterance, at others verse or aphorism.

There is nothing dull about this little bit of glass! One of its minor verses, which appeared to have the weight of far-seeing knowledge behind it, was, "People are just when men are Dust." Another little cryptic speech was, "When things are greenest there is oft decay."

Oh! the wisdom of the little tumbler! I have had many striking instances of the prophetic powers of this medium. A painful example of its clairvoyance was that once it spelt out " Beware of fire in old part of house." In less than a year after this warning, our house was burned down, the fire beginning apparently in the part of the house specified.

It also gave us information as to changes and complete alteration of plans, unthought of and most certainly not believed in at that time, but which were exactly carried out some months later. It foretold at some length a visit for the girl who was then touching the tumbler. She was going for the first time to some friends up in the North, the journey was described, a train being missed, and various other annoyances. Then it spelt out "A man in a pink coat will be at the station," which naturally seemed extremely improbable, but so it turned out to be; for the host had been hunting and had come in " pink " to meet his guest.

I give these few instances of the powers of the tumbler as a slight acknowledgement of its " uncanny," as it is often described, wisdom and foreknowledge. Let the readers try it for themselves, but to those who are beginning, it is very necessary to impress on them the need for patience. A great deal of this extremely useful quality may be needed. So much depends on the persons using the tumbler. It may begin to move or even write, at once, or it may be a long time, or what seems a very long time to those waiting, before it makes any movement at all. From whatever point of view it is regarded, whether as an amusement, or a means of translating knowledge desired to the everyday mind, it is worth while to be patient, for there is sure to be result.

It is quite likely that the tumbler, when it first begins to move, will make some rapid movements towards the letters, and you feel elated at its decisive activity, but it is also quite likely to turn back and retire to the point from whence it started, the centre of the table, and there remain, till a fresh impetus starts it off again. Do not get angry, it will gibber nonsense if you do!

To manipulate the tumbler under the easiest conditions, it is best to have two people *en rapport* — at any rate not antagonistic. It can also be done successfully with only one person touching it. I have stated I have seen excellent results when this has been the case, but it is certainly advisable to have two people for those who are experimenting.

We will now proceed to the method of using the tumbler.

The equipment needed is simple:—A good sized table, smooth it must be, or much difficulty occurs in the tumbler moving about freely. An ordinary glass tumbler, and the letters of the alphabet. The easiest plan for acquiring these is to buy the large printed letters on stiff squares, belonging to a game which is, I think, called "The Alphabet Game." If this is not obtainable, substitutes drawn on stiff paper do very well, but naturally the cardboard squares are better, they lie flat on the table, whereas the paper letters turn up and make it difficult to see which letter the tumbler is really pointing at. Also if there is any draught thin paper flutters about in a tiresome way.

Arrange the letters haphazard, not alphabetically, round the edge of the table; be sure not to put them too near to each other, for if you do it is very difficult to be certain of the letter the tumbler is seeking.

If the cardboard squares with the large printed letters on are not used, then make your alphabet on thick paper, and do not make the letters small.

Having arranged the letters round the edge of the table, put a tumbler upside down in the centre, then the two persons who are to make the experiment each place one finger on the bottom rim of the tumbler, the first or second finger is best, as being the most comfortable, but which finger is used is certainly a matter of individual taste. The finger must be held lightly on the glass, no pressure is needed and indeed it is undesirable, and would probably hinder the movements of the tumbler. If one of the persons touching it is more magnetic than the other, it is sure to draw the tumbler in that direction.

If the magnetism is strong the action will probably begin at once, and possibly all the conversations of the tumbler will be directed to that individual. But it may be that a great deal of patience will be necessary before any interesting developments occur. Do not be fussy or annoyed. If it seems quite hopeless (but this rarely happens) leave off and try again at another time. Do not attempt it when you are feeling tired. It is a great mistake. Being tired is not a fitting opportunity for giving out magnetism. Few things go at their best for a tired person, certainly the glass does not! It is a good plan, if enough interest is felt in this means of transmitting messages through the tumbler, for a third person to put down on a piece of paper the sentence spelt out. If the date is put down in connection with all remarks that appear to be prophetic, it is interesting to refer to afterwards and verify the events.

Of course there are people who assert that the tumbler is just pushed up to the letters, and this accounts for the remarks received. Of course it would be possible to receive messages like that especially when trivial remarks or statements are made, such as the delightful way of summing up the " flapper." Certainly to be impolite is not very difficult to some of us, but when it comes to warnings and statements of an entirely prophetic nature, of which no one in the room can have any conception, when it tells us of events not in the normal range of our knowledge, then indeed it would be entirely impossible to manipulate the tumbler in any way with hope of success.

What could be more utterly foolish than to try such a trick? If physical mechanism is needed, there can be no further interest in the tumbler. Why not play a game at once? This is one good reason for laying the finger as lightly as possible on the tumbler, then there cannot even be any unconscious effort to coerce it into moving in one direction or another. It is a good test for a third person to watch and take down the remarks of the tumbler, whilst those whose fingers are upon it should be blindfolded. They need not know till the sitting is finished what the subject of its disclosures was. Try this. It is quite a good plan for affording a convincing proof of the fact that all the tumbler does is to move from letter to letter, guided not by the fingers laid upon it, but by the subconscious power and knowledge within those who touch it.

Sometimes the tumbler's spelling is faulty,

it may even persist in spelling certain words from a system of its own, and with no attention to the rules of the English language. I have known it go back and try again if you point out that the spelling is not that to which you are accustomed. Sometimes no remonstrance has any effect, and the wrong spelling is persisted in, which seems to me an interesting fact.

If the tumbler appears to be trying to get at the name of a place or person, and the spelling of it leaves its identity quite uncertain, it is necessary then to beg the tumbler to try again and spell it more carefully. It usually does this and probably makes it clear to you. Occasionally its utterances are those of symbolism, and the meanings must be understood and interpreted by that language. At other times it is frankly bored, and boring, so entirely natural are its methods. Then again it may take you into the depths of despondency by its grey and gloomy views of life, or it may break out into a rollicking exuberance that leaves you feeling that nothing but the very best can ever happen in this best of all worlds. Once more it may lead you into such profound philosophies that you imagine it is reading from one of the greatest sages in history.

There is a marvelous variety in the conversations emanating from this simple source of knowledge, the common tumbler, but it must be remembered that it is, naturally, much influenced by those who are using it. For some people it does wonders, and for others only trivial nonsense results. Certainly it is worth a fair trial, and do not give up in despair if nothing satisfactory occurs during the first attempt or two. It is scarcely worth while to do anything which does not require a little patience and perseverance. The tumbler will not exact too much of either from you.

Of course it is a far easier method of divination than that of consulting the cards, and undoubtedly there are persons who will obtain through its mediumship all that they desire. When a critical moment in life comes, and the everyday normal mind is wearing itself out with anxiety over a difficult question, when there are no visible sign posts, then comes the moment to invoke the invisible and turn to one or other of those mediums I have described.

I would recommend both means of gaining subconscious knowledge being tried. Both are full of interest, and will yield substantial results. Here is a source of gaining information which is entirely at your own disposal, resulting in the case of the card readings especially, in giving much interest and assistance to others; with nothing more expensive to provide than a pack of cards.

This simple book will have satisfactorily carried out its purpose, if its readers become convinced of that wonderful power and knowledge hidden within us all and of which we may learn so much through the simple mediumship of card or tumbler.

THE END

CPSIA information can be obtained at www.ICGtesting.com
Printed in the USA
LVOW02*0340160813

348057LV00006B/56/P